Legalines®

Editorial Advisors:
Gloria A. Aluise
Attorney at Law
Jonathan Neville
Attorney at Law
Robert A. Wyler
Attorney at Law

Authors:
Gloria A. Aluise
Attorney at Law
Daniel O. Bernstine
Attorney at Law
Roy L. Brooks
Professor of Law
Scott M. Burbank
C.P.A.
Charles N. Carnes
Professor of Law
Paul S. Dempsey
Professor of Law
Jerome A. Hoffman
Professor of Law
Mark R. Lee
Professor of Law
Jonathan Neville
Attorney at Law
Laurence C. Nolan
Professor of Law
Arpiar Saunders
Attorney at Law
Robert A. Wyler
Attorney at Law

CRIMINAL LAW

Adaptable to Fourth Edition*
of Dressler Casebook

*If your casebook is a newer edition, go to www.gilbertlaw.com to see if a supplement is available for this title.

THOMSON
WEST

REGIONAL OFFICES: Chicago, Dallas, Los Angeles, New York, Washington, D.C.

SERIES EDITOR
Linda C. Schneider, J.D.
Attorney at Law

PRODUCTION MANAGER
Elizabeth G. Duke

FIRST PRINTING—2007

SHORT SUMMARY OF CONTENTS

TABLE OF CONTENTS AND SHORT REVIEW OUTLINE

I. INTRODUCTION: SETTING THE STAGE

A. NATURE, SOURCES, AND LIMITS OF THE CRIMINAL LAW

Criminal law can be characterized as a series of commands to act in a manner that our society has declared to be moral. A person who fails to obey these commands "will incur a formal and solemn pronouncement of the moral condemnation of the community" and be sanctioned.

Criminal law is rooted in common law. Over time, legislators took over the responsibility of defining criminal conduct, enacting criminal laws, and devising sanctions for disobedience. The legislators' authority, of course, is limited by federal and state constitutional law. The courts, in addition to passing on the constitutionality of criminal legislation, retain their role of interpreting the criminal law and ascertaining guilt or innocence under the law.

B. CRIMINAL LAW IN A PROCEDURAL CONTEXT: PRE-TRIAL

1. State Procedure.

a. **Offense.** The criminal justice system reacts to criminal conduct. The process begins when an offense is reported to the police. Investigators gather evidence—testimonial, tangible, or otherwise—with the objective of determining who perpetrated the crime. One significant procedural issue that frequently arises at this stage involves searches and seizures.

b. **Arrest.** Once sufficient evidence is gathered to constitute probable cause that an identified person committed the crime, the suspect may be arrested with or without a warrant, depending on the circumstances. The arresting officer takes the suspect into custody and brings him to the police station.

c. **The charge.** The police ask the district attorney to make out a formal charge and an affidavit, which is a written complaint charging the accused with a specified crime or crimes. A complaint is prepared in advance when a person is arrested under a warrant because it is used to obtain the warrant.

d. **Proceedings before a magistrate.** After arrest, the accused is taken before the committing magistrate (*e.g.*, a municipal court judge), who advises the accused of her rights and sends her back to jail or allows her to post bond. If the charge is a misdemeanor, the accused is immediately arraigned and must plead to the charge. If the charge is a felony, the accused normally does not have to plead; instead, a date is set for a preliminary hearing.

e. **Preliminary hearing.** When a felony is charged, the accused is entitled to a preliminary hearing to determine whether there are sufficient grounds to bind the accused over for a trial.

1) **Sufficient evidence.** The committing magistrate rules on the evidence. If the critical evidence is suppressed for some reason at this point, then the accused may be set free and the charge dismissed. The accused has a chance to cross-examine the prosecution's evidence, which is an important discovery technique.

2) **Decision.** If the committing magistrate finds that the evidence is sufficient, the accused is committed.

3) **Writ of prohibition.** If the magistrate finds sufficient evidence, the accused may bring a writ of prohibition to appeal the magistrate's findings.

f. **Indictment.** As an alternative to a preliminary hearing, the prosecution may seek an indictment. The prosecuting attorney presents a written accusation to an investigatory body, such as a grand jury. An indictment is simply a finding made by the grand jury that there is sufficient evidence to warrant a conviction of the crime. A grand jury indictment may either precede or follow arrest. The prosecution may choose the indictment procedure when it wants to keep its information confidential, because in most states the accused does not have the opportunity to appear or to challenge the prosecution's evidence.

g. **Accusatory pleading.** The prosecution of the case commences once the government files either an indictment or an information. An information is simply the written charge on which the accused will be tried.

h. **Arraignment.** Once the pleading is filed, the accused is brought before the court and informed of the charge(s). The accused then pleads to the charge(s).

i. **Motions and pleas.** The accused is normally permitted to make certain motions or one of several different pleas.

1) **Motions.** The accused may file a demurrer, or a challenge to the legal sufficiency of the accusatory pleading, such as that the court lacks jurisdiction or that no crime is alleged. Other motions include ones to quash or set aside the indictment or information, to dismiss, to change venue to another court, to obtain discovery, or to suppress certain evidence.

2) **Pleas.** If the charges hold up after consideration of the motions, the accused may plead guilty, not guilty, or nolo contendere, which is the same as pleading guilty except that the conviction cannot be used in subsequent civil proceedings.

j. **Discovery.** Normally, both sides continue the fact-finding process to prepare for trial. The parties use the discovery process to find out as much as possible about the opposition's case.

k. **Extraordinary writs.** The accused may file certain extraordinary writs before trial begins. The writ of prohibition is an appeal to a higher court to terminate the judicial process, normally on the basis of a lack of proper jurisdiction in the lower court. The other writ in common use is that of habeas corpus ("bring forth the body"), which tests any restraint that is contrary to "fundamental law," *e.g.*, the state constitution.

2. **Federal Procedure.**

a. **Similarities to state procedure.** In many respects, federal criminal procedure resembles state procedure. In fact, the Federal Rules of Evidence and Federal Rules of Criminal Procedure ("Fed. R. Crim. P.") have served as models for state procedure. A few of the significant rules are discussed below. (Remember that only federal crimes are prosecuted in the federal system.)

b. **Arrest.** A warrant may be issued on presentation of a complaint by the United States Attorney, identifying the crime and the accused. [Fed. R. Crim. P. 4(a)] A valid arrest may also be made without a warrant where there is probable cause.

c. **Appearance before a magistrate.** If the accused was arrested without a warrant, then a complaint is prepared. If a warrant was used, the complaint was previously prepared. The accused is next brought before a magistrate. This must be done without unnecessary delay. [Fed. R. Crim. P. 5(a)]

d. **Preliminary examination.** Preliminary examinations are also held before a magistrate. [Fed. R. Crim. P. 5(c)]

e. **Grand jury indictment.** If a grand jury has returned an indictment against the accused, he is not entitled to a preliminary examination, except that Fed. R. Crim. P. 5(c) provides that if a person is taken into custody before the indictment is given, he is entitled to a preliminary examination. This avoids the problem of a lengthy holding of a defendant waiting for a grand jury.

f. **Arraignment.** The accused is arraigned in federal district court.

g. **Motions and pleas.** Under Fed. R. Crim. P. 12, the motion to dismiss is used in place of all other motions discussed above under state procedure. This motion attacks all possible defects.

C. CRIMINAL LAW IN A PROCEDURAL CONTEXT: TRIAL BY JURY

1. **Trial.** Numerous procedural issues arise during the trial process, including the following:

   a. The competency of the accused to stand trial, as well as the sanity of the accused at the time of the offense;

   b. The accused's right to counsel;

   c. The right to trial by jury and the selection of jurors;

   d. The right to a fair trial;

   e. The accused's and the witnesses' privilege against self-incrimination, including the accused's right not to testify as a witness at all;

   f. The right to compulsory process to obtain witnesses;

   g. The right to confront accusers and cross-examine witnesses;

   h. Issues relating to trial of two or more accused persons in the same trial, to more than one trial of the same accused for the same criminal act, and to the trial of the same accused for more than one crime arising from the same act;

   i. Evidence questions relating to the introduction or order of evidence, the burden of proof, motions, jury instructions, etc.; and

   j. The verdict, the sentence, and the entry of judgment by the court.

2. **Jury.**

   a. The jury's responsibility. The jury has the responsibility of hearing all the evidence, receiving instructions from the judge about the law, and then applying the law in finding facts and making the ultimate decision of guilt or innocence.

   b. Constitutional provisions.

   1) Article III, Section 2. "The trial of all Crimes, except in Cases of Impeachment, shall be by jury . . . ."

   2) Sixth Amendment. "In all criminal prosecutions, the accused shall enjoy the right to speedy and public trial, by an impartial jury of the State and district wherein the crime shall have been committed."

3) **Effect.** By virtue of Article III, Section 2 and the Sixth Amendment, a defendant charged in a federal court with any serious offense (as distinguished from a "petty" offense under the common law) is entitled to trial by jury.

4) **Serious vs. petty offenses.** Because the Sixth Amendment guarantees a jury trial only when a serious offense is charged, it becomes necessary to distinguish between "serious" and "petty" offenses. The court looks to the nature of the offense and the maximum potential sentence.

c. **Number of jurors.** The number of jurors in federal criminal trials is 12, but this is by statute [Fed. R. Crim. P. 23] and is not constitutionally required. State rules allowing use of fewer than 12 jurors (in noncapital cases) have been upheld. [Williams v. Florida, 399 U.S. 78 (1970)]

d. **Impartial jury.** Safeguards have been put in place to ensure that a jury is indeed impartial. The jury pool is drawn from a fair sampling of the community. During voir dire, the judge and the lawyers examine each potential juror to determine whether he is impartial, *i.e.*, whether his attitudes and beliefs regarding the particular issues or parties involved would prevent him from following the law. The parties are also allowed to exercise peremptory challenges, excluding persons from the jury for reasons other than proven impartiality. The Equal Protection Clause of the Fourteenth Amendment prohibits peremptory challenges based on gender or race.

D. PROOF OF GUILT AT TRIAL

1. Proof Beyond a Reasonable Doubt.

a. **Standard of proof.** Generally, the factfinder in a civil trial may base its findings on a preponderance of the evidence. In criminal trials, however, the defendant is presumed innocent. Therefore, to convict, a jury must find the defendant guilty beyond a reasonable doubt. The conviction must be based on proof beyond a reasonable doubt of every fact required to make up the crime charged. This high standard of proof reflects the serious consequences of a criminal conviction, which should not attach to a person when there is a reasonable doubt about guilt.

b. **Use of presumptions.** Presumptions may allow a factfinder to infer a fact not proved from a fact actually proved. This evidentiary sense of the term is distinct from the term when used, for example, in the phrase, "presumed innocent until proven guilty." The latter usage merely is a way to state that the prosecution must prove guilt. The evidentiary presumptions, however, may allow the prosecution to prove guilt without actually proving every critical fact, when permissible inferences may be drawn from the facts proved.

2. Enforcing the Presumption of Innocence--

Owens v. State, 611 A.2d 1043 (Md. 1992).

Facts. A state trooper investigating a complaint of a suspicious vehicle found Owens (D) in a truck parked in the driveway of a private residence. Whether the residence was D's is not in evidence. The truck's engine was running and its lights were on, D was asleep with an open beer can between his legs, and two more empty beer cans were inside the truck. When the trooper awakened him, D appeared intoxicated. The trooper also discovered that D had an alcohol restriction on his license. D was charged and ultimately convicted of driving while intoxicated, based solely on circumstantial evidence. D appeals.

Issue. Was D's conviction, based upon circumstantial evidence alone, legally sufficient?

Held. Yes. Judgment affirmed.

- A conviction upon circumstantial evidence alone should not be sustained unless the circumstances are inconsistent with any reasonable hypothesis of innocence. From D's presence behind the wheel of a vehicle on a driveway with its lights on and motor running, it can reasonably be inferred that D had either just arrived by way of the public highway or was about to set forth upon the public highway. The first inference would render D guilty; the second would not. A "tiebreaking" factor must enhance the likelihood of one inference while diminishing the likelihood of the other.

- The presence of the opened beer can between D's legs and the empty cans on the floor give rise to a reasonable inference that D's trip was concluding rather than beginning when the trooper found him, as one does not typically drink in the house and then carry the empty cans to the car. Furthermore, D's unconscious state suggests that D had not just begun to drink, and it is unlikely that D turned on the truck and then drank enough to pass out before beginning to drive. Moreover, the fact that the police were called to investigate a suspicious vehicle suggests that the vehicle had been observed moving in an erratic manner as opposed to just sitting, with its motor idling, in a driveway.

- While none of the evidence proves guilt in and of itself, the totality of the circumstances are inconsistent with a reasonable hypothesis of innocence. The circumstances diminish the likelihood that D is innocent while enhancing the likelihood of his guilt. Thus, D's conviction was legally sufficient.

E. JURY NULLIFICATION

1. **Introduction.** Even if a prosecutor proves a case beyond a reasonable doubt, the jury has the power to ignore the facts and the judge's instructions and sim-

ply acquit for any reason. Jurors might choose to do so based on their feelings about the law, the circumstances, the accused, etc. The power of juries is evident from the Fifth Amendment Double Jeopardy Clause's bar on the retrial of a defendant after a jury acquittal. Questions arise as to whether juries should nullify the law and whether they should be informed that they may nullify the law.

2. **Nullification Is Unfortunate but Unavoidable--**

State v. Ragland, 519 A.2d 1361 (N.J. 1986).

Facts. Ragland (D) was tried for possession of a weapon by a convicted felon. At the trial's conclusion, the judge instructed the jury that it "must find him guilty of the [possession] charge" if it found that D had possessed a weapon while committing a robbery. D was convicted. D appeals, asserting in part that the judge's use of the word "must" in his instructions conflicted with the jury's power to nullify the law and contending that the jury should have been informed of its right to nullify.

Issue. Should a jury be instructed on its power of nullification?

Held. No. Judgment reversed on other grounds.

- ♦ By virtue of the finality of an acquittal verdict, a jury simply has the power to nullify the law. It is nothing more than a power; it is not one of the attributes of a right to trial by jury. The exercise of this power is undesirable. Our style of government is based in part on the belief that only our elected officials may determine what is a crime and what is not, and only those officials may revise the law—not a group of random people in a jury box. There is no constitutional or legal authority mandating this proposed change in standard jury instructions.

- ♦ Public policy also weighs against such a change. Nullification is the power to act against the law. It allows the jury to act arbitrarily. Advising jurors of the law and then of their power to ignore it would be confusing, at best. The power of nullification is absolutely inconsistent with the most important value of democracy, that we should live under a government of laws and not of men.

Comment. In *United States v. Datcher*, 830 F. Supp. 411 (M.D. Tenn. 1993), Judge Thomas Wiseman, Jr., wrote that the Constitution's drafters "clearly intended [the right of trial by jury] to protect the accused from oppression by the Government," using as an example the power of jury nullification absent which, in his opinion, judicial tyranny not only is a possibility, but was and remains a reality. "Judicial and prosecutorial excesses still occur, and Congress is not yet an infallible body incapable of making tyrannical laws."

II. PRINCIPLES OF PUNISHMENT

A. THEORIES OF PUNISHMENT

1. **Introduction.** Criminal laws are enacted in recognition of the fact that certain types of conduct have the effect of disrupting social order and infringe on the rights of others. Some form of punishment is affixed to violations of the criminal laws, but the justification for such punishment is not always apparent.

2. **Deterrence.**

   a. **Introduction.** Punishment serves many functions for society. One belief of penologists is that, by punishing those who commit acts condemned by society, others will be deterred from committing similar acts, for fear of the punishment that will result from their acts.

   b. **Value structure.** Society's demand that certain acts be punished expresses its collective belief in the wrongfulness of some acts. Failure to punish these wicked acts has the effect of endorsing acts that are contrary to society's value structure of what is right and what is wrong.

   c. **Social embarrassment as a deterrent.** Social embarrassment is one of many forms of deterrence (antitrust violators suffer social disgrace, for example). In other words, the sentence means little, but the conviction means a lot. And, in murder cases, an indictment alone is often as much of a stigma as would be a conviction of some other crimes.

   d. **Summary comments on deterrence.** Deterrence theories furnish the most widely accepted rationale of the practice of punishment. According to these theories, punishment should not be designed to exact retribution upon convicted offenders, but to deter the commission of future offenses. However, most studies indicate that severity of punishment has only a slight effect in deterring crime. For example, white-collar business crimes and drug trafficking are two types of crimes for which there is no evidence that fear of lengthy incarceration affects any significant number of criminal decisions. More important in deterring crime is increased certainty of arrest, conviction, and imprisonment. Certainty and severity of punishment together operate as the most effective deterrents of crime. Either one alone is ineffective.

3. **Retribution.** Retribution focuses primarily on the nature of the offense and its condemnation by society. This theory of punishment states that a criminal must be punished for the "wrong he has committed." Retribution looks to the past, not to the future, and rests solely upon the foundation of vindictive justice, *i.e.*, "an eye for an eye." There are numerous versions of the retribution theory. "Positive retribution" is the view that innocent people may never be punished

and that guilty people must always be punished. "Negative retribution" is the view that it is morally wrong to impose punishment on innocent people even if the punishment would benefit society. "Assaultive retribution" is the view that criminals should be hated and that their punishments should reflect that hatred. "Protective retribution" is the view that criminals have a right to have punishment imposed on them for their choice to violate the rules of society.

4. **Rehabilitation.** In addition to retribution and crime deterrence, penology also seeks to reform the criminal to become a useful member of society. However, it would be a paradox if the main purpose of providing punishment for murder was to reform the murderer, not to prevent murder. Yet rehabilitation is an important, though elusive, goal.

5. **Segregation.** An additional goal of the criminal law is to protect society by segregating the criminal offender from general society, thereby limiting the number of people against whom he can commit further crimes.

6. **Summary.** The purpose of the criminal law is to protect the public interest by preventing certain undesirable conduct. Views of the differing theories of punishment have varied greatly, and penology is in constant tension between the purposes or ends it seeks to serve. Should deterrence be given supremacy? Should rehabilitation? Should retribution? Retribution has little support today, while rehabilitation, at least in theory, has become a chief goal of penology.

B. THE PENAL THEORIES IN ACTION

1. Who Should Be Punished?--

The Queen v. Dudley and Stephens, 14 Q.B.D. 273 (1884).

Facts. Dudley was the captain, and Stephens, Brooks, and Parker were crew members on a yacht. A storm forced them to abandon ship in an open lifeboat with no food or water. They were lost at sea for many days. After several days without food, Dudley and Stephens (Ds) spoke to Brooks about killing Parker, an eighteen-year-old boy who was weaker than the others. Ds, who both had families, wanted to kill and eat Parker so that they might survive. Brooks refused to take part in the plot, but Dudley, with Stephens's consent, cut the boy's throat, and all three men fed upon the body. The three men were rescued four days later, and Ds were charged with murder. A jury found that: had the men not fed upon Parker's body, they would probably have died; Parker was in a much weaker condition than the rest of them and was likely to have died before any of the others; and Parker's death was not due to any violence on his part against the others. The jury could not decide whether Ds were guilty of murder under these circumstances, and the decision was referred to be argued before a panel of five judges.

Issue. Are Ds guilty of murder under these circumstances?

Held. Yes. Ds convicted of murder.

- Ds argue that Parker would likely have died first anyway because he was already much more severely weakened by starvation than the others. Ds further argue that they too would have died had they not eaten his flesh over the final four days of their ordeal. Finally, Ds argue that one does not commit murder when he kills to save his own life. We find these facts are no legal justification for murder.

- It is true that taking the life of another in self-defense is justified. However, in this case, Ds were not acting in self-defense. Parker presented no threat to anyone's life. The only way the killing could be justified is if it were done by "necessity." However, we find that there is no absolute or unqualified necessity to save one's own life. The weakest, most vulnerable crew member was chosen to be killed. It cannot be said that it was more necessary to kill him than any of the others.

- While we are sympathetic to the terrible suffering of Ds during this ordeal at sea, we cannot allow compassion for Ds to change or weaken in any manner the legal definition of murder. We find Ds guilty of murder.

---

2. How Much (and What) Punishment Should Be Imposed?

a. Suspended sentences and probation--

People v. Du, No. BA037738 (Super. Ct., Los Angeles County 1991).

Facts. [Facts excerpted from *People v. Superior Court*, 5 Cal. App. 4th 822, 7 Cal. Rptr. 2d 177 (1992)] Du (D) and her family owned and operated two liquor stores. Although D usually worked at her other store, on the day in question, D was working at her Empire Liquor Market store in place of her son, who had been threatened at Empire Liquor by local gang members. The store had been burglarized numerous times, shoplifting occurred frequently, and the store had been threatened with arson. D was working alone in the store when she observed fifteen-year-old Latasha Harlins enter the store, take a bottle of juice from the refrigerator, and put it in her backpack. Although Harlins then approached the counter with two or three dollars in her hand, D knew from experience that shoplifters often hid merchandise on their person and then approached the counter to buy a few smaller items, so she confronted Harlins. Witnesses testified that Harlins stated that she would pay for the juice. However, D said that when she asked Harlins to pay for the orange juice, Harlins asked, "What orange juice?" A struggle ensued, culminating in Harlins punching D and then D reaching for a gun under the counter and killing Harlins. The gun had previously been stolen from D's family and had been returned in an altered state, making it fire with virtually no effort. The jury found D guilty of use of a gun in the commission of a felony as well as voluntary manslaughter, rejecting the defenses that the killing was unintentional and that D acted in self-defense. In the sentencing phase, the judge considered the facts of the case along with a presentence probation report characterizing D as "most unlikely to repeat this or any other crime if she were allowed to remain free. . . . She is not a person who would actively seek to harm another."

Issue. Are a suspended sentence and probation appropriate?

Held. Yes. Ten-year prison sentence imposed but suspended, with D placed on probation.

- The objectives of sentencing a defendant are to protect society, to punish, to encourage the defendant to lead a law-abiding life, to deter others, to prevent further crimes, to secure restitution for the victim, and to seek uniformity in sentencing. Under the facts of this case, none of these sentencing objectives would truly be served by incarcerating D.

- There is a presumption against probation when a firearm is used. The statute, however, is aimed at criminals who arm themselves to commit crimes, not at shopkeepers who lawfully possess weapons for protection. Additionally, D has no record of similar crimes or crimes of violence. Furthermore, D committed the crime under circumstances of great provocation, coercion, and duress, due to the crime and fear to which her family had been subjected recently. Thus, the presumption is overcome.

- Finally, there is no evidence that D knew that the gun had been altered when she picked it up to use in self-defense. D testified that she had never held a gun before, that she did not know how it worked, and that she had not intended to kill Harlins.

---

b. Shaming--

United States v. Gementera, 379 F.3d 596 (9th Cir. 2004).

Facts. Gementera (D) pled guilty to mail theft. Although D was only 24 years old, he already had a long criminal record. The judge sentenced D to two months of incarceration and three years of supervised release. One condition of his release was that D perform 100 hours of community service by standing in front of a postal facility wearing a sandwich board reading "I stole mail. This is my punishment." D's sentence was later modified to require that D wear the sign for only eight hours, but also required that D observe postal patrons visiting the "lost or missing mail" window, write letters of apology to any identifiable victims of his crime, and deliver several lectures at a local high school. D appeals.

Issue. Does the release condition requiring D to wear a sandwich board publicly announcing his crime violate the Sentencing Reform Act?

Held. No. Judgment affirmed.

- The Sentencing Reform Act affords courts broad discretion in fashioning conditions of supervised release. Such conditions must serve legitimate objectives and be reasonably related to the nature of the offense and the history of the defendant. The three legitimate statutory purposes are (i) deterrence, (ii) protection of the public, and (iii) rehabilitation. Any condition imposed must be reasonably related to these purposes. Thus, in analyzing any particular condition, the court must determine whether the sentencing judge imposed the condition for a permissible purpose and whether the condition is reasonably related to that purpose.

- Here, D argues that the sandwich board condition was imposed for the impermissible purpose of humiliation. Although humiliation will be a likely result of the condition, humiliation itself was not the point. The court's order stressed that public exposure of D's crime and exposure of D to his victims was to serve the primary purpose of rehabilitation and also to have a deterrent effect on both D and others in the community.

- These are legitimate purposes. Thus, the next prong of the test is whether the condition imposed was "reasonably related" to those purposes. D argues that no scientific evidence shows that shaming is rehabilitative. However, all criminal offenses and the penalties that accompany them cause shame and embarrassment. Such feelings signal a defendant's acknowledgement of his wrongdoing.

- Furthermore, the sandwich board condition was not a stand-alone condition. D was also required to write apologies to his victims and lecture at a high school. All of these conditions together were tailored to the specific needs of D and are reasonably related to his rehabilitation.

Dissent. The shaming punishment at issue here was intended to humiliate D, and that is all that it will do. Humiliation is not one of the three proper goals under the Sentencing Reform Act. The trial judge clearly stated that D should have to suffer "humiliation." Deterrence and rehabilitation are merely retroactive justifications for the punishment. As far as the other conditions, humiliation does not cease to be humiliation just because it is paired with other punishments. Finally, this decision is bad policy. Such punishment recalls the history of "pillories and stocks," and by sanctioning such use of power, we run the risk of instilling disrespect for the criminal justice system.

Comment. In the United States, criminal punishment generally involves imprisonment. "Shaming" is a creative alternative form of sentencing that may involve stigmatizing publicity, public contrition, or public humiliation. Under another alternative, known as "restorative justice," the goal is an interpersonal reconciliation between the offender and his victim, as well as a social reconciliation between the wrongdoer and the community. This type of justice is more often used in cases involving property offenses than violent crimes and is generally used only if both the offender and the victim choose to pursue this alternative.

C. PROPORTIONALITY OF PUNISHMENT

1. **General Principles.** Legislators strive to ensure that punishments are proportionate to the crimes. The courts must defer to legislative judgments as to what punishments are appropriate, but only up to a point; if the punishment is outrageously disproportionate in a given case, the courts may forbid enforcement of the punishment.

2. **Constitutional Principles.**

    a. **Cruel and unusual punishment.** The Eighth Amendment prohibits cruel and unusual punishment. This prohibition applies to inherently cruel punishments such as torture and execution by painful and lingering methods. It also prohibits punishments that, while conceptually permissible, are cruel and unusual in a given case because the punishment is so disproportionate to the crime.

    b. **Death penalty--**

Coker v. Georgia, 433 U.S. 584 (1977).

Facts. Coker (D), who was imprisoned for murder, rape, kidnaping, and aggravated assault, escaped from prison. He entered the Carvers' house through an unlocked door, threatened them, tied the husband up, took the husband's money and car keys, threatened the wife's life with a knife from the kitchen, raped the wife, and drove away in the Carvers' car with the wife. After freeing himself, the husband notified police, D was apprehended, and the wife suffered no further harm. D was charged with escape, armed robbery, motor vehicle theft, kidnaping, and rape, and the jury found him guilty. At the sentencing phase, the jury was instructed that the death penalty could be imposed for the rape if one of specific aggravating circumstances were found. They were also instructed that they need not impose the death penalty, even if an aggravating circumstance were found, if they determined that the circumstance was outweighed by a mitigating circumstance that in fairness or mercy reduced the degree of moral culpability or punishment. The jury found two aggravating circumstances—that D had a prior felony conviction and that the rape was committed during the course of another capital felony—and sentenced D to death. D appealed, the Georgia Supreme Court affirmed, and the United States Supreme Court granted certiorari on D's claim that his sentence constituted cruel and unusual punishment under the Eighth Amendment.

Issue. Is the death penalty cruel and unusual punishment for the rape of an adult?

Held. Yes. Judgment reversed.

- The death penalty is not invariably cruel and unusual punishment. It is unconstitutional, however, if it (i) makes no measurable contribution to acceptable goals of punishment, and hence is nothing more than purposeless and needless imposition of pain and suffering, or (ii) is grossly disproportionate to the severity of the crime.

- Rape, while highly reprehensible and deserving of serious punishment, does not compare with murder. The death penalty is excessive for the rapist who does not take a human life. D's prior conviction for murder does not change the fact that the instant crime did not involve the taking of a life.

Concurrence (Brennan, Marshall, JJ.). The death penalty always constitutes cruel and unusual punishment.

Concurrence and dissent (Powell, J.). Under the circumstances of this case, as well as ordinarily, death is a disproportionate sentence for the crime of raping an adult woman. It was unnecessary, however, for the plurality to foreclose the death penalty for the crime of rape under any circumstance not involving the taking of life.

Dissent (Burger, C.J., Rehnquist, J.). The Eighth Amendment does not prevent a state from taking an individual's "well-demonstrated propensity for life-endangering behavior" into account in devising sentences that will prevent inflicting further harm on innocent victims. D is a chronic rapist whose continuing danger to the community is abundantly clear. Rape causes serious psychological and physical harm and is likely to have an irreparable long-range effect on the victim's life. There is no constitutional prohibition to imposing the death penalty under some circumstances involving rape.

---

c. "Three strikes" laws--

Ewing v. California, 538 U.S. 11 (2003).

Facts. Ewing (D) was a repeat felon who had been convicted of numerous misdemeanors and felonies, including robbery and residential burglary. While on parole from a nine-year prison term, D stole three golf clubs worth $399 each from a pro shop. He was convicted of felony grand theft and sentenced to 25 years to life under California's "three strikes" law. D appeals his sentence, arguing that it is disproportionate and violates the Eight Amendment's prohibition of cruel and unusual punishment. D argues that, under California law, grand theft is one of several crimes known as "wobblers," meaning that they may be classified as felonies or misdemeanors. Thus, if theft of the golf clubs (the offense that "triggered" the three strikes law) had been treated as a misdemeanor, D would not have been sentenced under the three strikes law. The United States Supreme

Court granted certiorari to determine whether D's sentence violated the Eighth Amendment.

Issue. Does the Eighth Amendment prohibit a state from sentencing a repeat felon to a prison term of 25 years to life under its "Three Strikes and You're Out" law?

Held. No.

- Under California's three strikes law, a defendant who is convicted of a felony and has two or more prior "serious" or "violent" felony convictions must be sentenced to "an indeterminate term of life imprisonment" with no eligibility for parole for at least 25 years. While noting that the Eighth Amendment prohibits imposition of a sentence grossly disproportionate to the severity of the crime, this Court has previously upheld this type of recidivism statute. In *Rummel v. Estelle,* 445 U.S. 263 (1980), we held that sentencing a three-time offender to life imprisonment with the possibility of parole did not violate the Eighth Amendment. However, in *Solem v. Helm*, 463 U.S. 277 (1983), we held that the Eighth Amendment prohibited a life sentence without possibility of parole for a seventh nonviolent felony. In *Solem*, we set out three factors relevant to determining whether a sentence is so disproportionate that it violates the Eighth Amendment. The court must consider: (i) the gravity of the offense and the severity of the penalty, (ii) the sentences of other criminals in the same jurisdiction, and (iii) the sentences imposed for the same crime in other jurisdictions. In a later case, *Harmelin v. Michigan*, 501 U.S. 957 (1991), which did not involve recidivism, we explained that the Eighth Amendment does not require strict proportionality between the offense and the sentence, but prohibits sentences that are "grossly disproportionate" to the offense.

- Traditionally, this Court has deferred to legislative policy choices in this area because the Constitution does not require adoption of any specific penological theory. A prison sentence can have a variety of justifications including retribution, deterrence, incapacitation, and rehabilitation. The California legislature has determined that public safety requires incapacitating repeat criminals, and the Eighth Amendment does not prohibit that choice.

- In weighing the gravity of D's offense, we must consider his long history of felony recidivism. He had been convicted previously of "serious" or "violent" felonies. The fact that grand theft is a "wobbler" in the state is of no consequence. California courts have authority to exercise discretion to treat grand theft as a misdemeanor, but grand theft is presumptively a felony unless the court chooses to exercise this discretion.

- D is a repeat criminal who has been previously convicted of serious crimes, including first-degree robbery and residential burglary. During one of those robberies, D threatened his victim with a knife. His lengthy sentence is justified by the state's judgment that offenders who have committed serious or violent felonies and continue to commit felonies must be incapacitated. We therefore hold that

D's sentence of 25 years to life is not disproportionate and does not violate the Eighth Amendment.

Concurrence (Scalia, J.). Proportionality can only logically be tied to the penological goal of retribution, not to deterrence or rehabilitation. The Court should read the Eighth Amendment as stating that all punishment should reasonably pursue the multiple purposes of the criminal law instead of inferring the unstated requirement that punishment be reasonably proportionate to the gravity of the offense.

Concurrence (Thomas, J.). The Cruel and Unusual Punishment Clause of the Eighth Amendment does not contain a proportionality principle.

Dissent (Breyer, Stevens, Souter, Ginsburg, JJ.).

- The critical difference between the *Rummel* case, where the Court upheld a recidivist's sentence, and the *Solem* case, where the Court struck down a recidivist's sentence, was the length of the prison term. In terms of the value of the property stolen, D's case is closer to *Rummel*. However, in terms of the length of the sentence, D's case is closer to *Solem*. The sentence in *Rummel* amounted to 10 to 12 years in real time. As in *Solem*, the sentence here is long enough to constitute the productive remainder of almost any offender's life. *Solem* requires us to consider the harm to society caused or threatened by the crime, "the absolute magnitude of the crime," and the offender's culpability. Here, the crime triggering the sentencing was shoplifting, which, while serious in terms of the cost to retailers, is less serious than much other criminal conduct. These factors make D's gross disproportionality argument a strong one.

- A comparative analysis of D's sentence with sentencing practices in other jurisdictions and in California, outside the three strikes context, reveals that D's recidivist sentence is unique in its harshness.

- Finally, I fail to see how D's sentence can further a significant criminal justice objective. The stated objective of this particular three strikes law is to reduce serious and violent crime. Imposition of this sentence does not serve that objective. It only serves to incapacitate D.

III. MODERN ROLE OF CRIMINAL STATUTES

A. PRINCIPLE OF LEGALITY

1. **Previously Defined Conduct.** Statutes should give fair warning of what conduct is prohibited. Some statutes that fail to define clearly the prohibitions have been held to be void for vagueness. Certainty is a desired feature of any system of law, but it is not always possible to precisely define illegal conduct.

   a. **Fair warning.**

      1) **Common law.** At common law, absent a statute, the only conduct that was criminal was that which was deemed malum in se (inherently evil). The common law took a theological approach, which looked at the intrinsic quality of conduct.

      2) **Criminal codes.** One of the reasons for the formulation of criminal codes is to safeguard conduct that is without fault from arbitrary condemnation as criminal and to give fair warning of the nature of the conduct that does constitute a criminal offense.

   b. **What constitutes a crime?--**

Commonwealth v. Mochan, 110 A.2d 788 (Penn. 1955).

Facts. Over a period of time, Mochan (D) telephoned Zivkovich, a stranger to him and a married woman of high character and repute, as often as three times a week and at any hour of the day or night. On these occasions, he would talk to her in an obscene manner, solicit sexual intercourse and sodomy, and otherwise speak offensively. D's conduct was not prohibited by any statute, but D was charged under common law principles with intending "to debauch and corrupt, and further devising and intending to harass, embarrass and villify [sic]" the victim and her family. D was tried, convicted, and sentenced by a judge without a jury. D appeals on the ground that his conduct does not constitute a misdemeanor at common law.

Issue. Can D be convicted under common law for actions that are not criminal offenses by statute?

Held. Yes. Judgment affirmed.

- Even if there is no exact precedent, common law principles dictate that any act which injuriously affects public morality is a misdemeanor at common law.

- D's outrageously indecent behavior rises above the level of merely attempting to persuade a married woman to commit adultery. Furthermore, D's actions at least potentially injuriously affected public morality, as at least two persons in the victim's household heard some of D's language and the operator or anyone else on D's four-party telephone line could have listened in on the conversations. Thus, the facts of this case identify the offense as a common law misdemeanor.

Dissent. While D's conduct was reprehensible, under our system of government, it is for the legislature to determine what constitutes a crime.

---

c. **Death of an unborn fetus--**

Keeler v. Superior Court, 470 P.2d 617 (Cal. 1970).

Facts. Five months after receiving a divorce, Keeler (D) saw his former wife, who was pregnant by another man. According to medical testimony, the wife was 35 weeks pregnant, and the fetus would have had a 75% to 96% chance of survival if born at that time. D kicked his former wife in the stomach, and the baby was born dead. D was charged with murder. The action is a proceeding for a writ of prohibition.

Issue. May a person be guilty of murder for killing an unborn fetus when the law has not determined whether an unborn fetus is a "human being"?

Held. No. Writ should issue.

- The settled meaning of the term "human being" is a person born alive. Thus, D's act is not covered by current statute.
- There are no common law crimes in California.
- Due process prevents retroactive application of a penal statute even if the court had the power to rule that a fetus is a "human being."

Dissent. Medicine now makes it possible for most viable fetuses to be born alive. This fact should be taken into account in interpreting the statute.

---

d. **Ex post facto laws.** Without statutory authority, judicial determination that certain conduct is criminal deprives a defendant of fair warning by making that which was previously noncriminal into a punishable criminal act. This is the definition of an ex post facto law. The United States Constitution prohibits both state and federal governments from passing such laws.

2. **The Values of Statutory Clarity.**

   a. **Introduction.** The law should be certain enough so that persons who want to determine the legality of their conduct can do so without acting and then being held responsible for something they believed permissible.

   b. **"Peeping Tom" statute--**

In re **Banks,** 244 S.E.2d 386 (N.C. 1978).

Facts. Banks (D) was charged under a "Peeping Tom" statute that provides that "[a]ny person who shall peep secretly into any room occupied by a female person shall be guilty of a misdemeanor and upon conviction shall be fined or imprisoned in the discretion of the court." The trial court found that the statute is unconstitutionally vague. The State appeals.

Issue. Does the statute violate the Due Process Clause of the Fourteenth Amendment because it is unconstitutionally vague or overly broad?

Held. No. The statute is not unconstitutional.

- The requirement that a statute be definite remedies the evils of lack of fair notice of the conduct prohibited and the failure to define a reasonably ascertainable standard of guilt. We begin with the presumption that the statute is constitutional. If the statute is susceptible to two interpretations, only one of which is constitutional, the court should adopt the interpretation resulting in a finding of constitutionality.

- When the language of a statute is clear and unambiguous, the court must give the statute its plain and definite meaning. Where the statute is ambiguous or unclear, the court must interpret the language to give effect to the legislative intent. To do so, the court may look to such indicia as the purposes appearing from the statute as a whole, the phraseology, the law upon which the statute was based, the mischief to be remedied, the preamble, the title, the legislative history, and previous interpretations of same or similar statutes.

- The "Peeping Tom" statute was derived from the common law crimes of nuisance and eavesdropping. The words "Peeping Tom" are commonly understood in our country to mean a person who sneaks up to a window and peeps for the purpose of spying on an inhabitant and invading her privacy. Previous cases dealing with this statute involved conduct within the purview of the common usage of the term "Peeping Tom." A previous case dealing with the statute indicated that the word "secretly" conveys the idea of spying on another with the intention of invading her privacy. The language of the statute is sufficient to inform a person of ordinary intelligence of the acts the statute seeks to prohibit.

- The statute is not overbroad, as it requires that the offender be spying for the wrongful purpose of invading a female victim's privacy, thereby excluding from its scope persons who have a legitimate purpose to their actions or who inadvertently glance in another's window.

---

c. **Gang loitering statute--**

City of Chicago v. Morales, 527 U.S. 41 (1999).

Facts. The City of Chicago's (D's) "Gang Congregation Ordinance" barred "criminal street gang members" from "loitering" with one another or with other persons in any public place. Violation of the statute required that: (i) a police officer must reasonably believe that at least one of the people present in a public place is a gang member; (ii) the persons must be loitering, *i.e.*, "remaining in any one place with no apparent purpose"; (iii) the officer must order all of the persons to disperse and leave the area; and (iv) a person must disobey the officer's order. Any person who refused to leave, whether or not a gang member, was guilty of violating the ordinance. The United States Supreme Court granted certiorari to determine the constitutionality of the ordinance.

Issue. Does the ordinance violate the Due Process Clause of the Fourteenth Amendment because it is unconstitutionally vague?

Held. Yes.

- The ordinance goes beyond prohibiting intimidating conduct by gang members upon the public. It broadly covers a significant amount of activity, but there is uncertainty about the scope of that coverage.
- Vagueness will invalidate a law if: (i) it fails to provide notice that would be understood by ordinary citizens, and (ii) it is susceptible to arbitrary and discriminatory enforcement.
- The ordinance does not give notice because its definition of "loiter" is not a commonly accepted definition. The statute fails to provide a standard by which the police can judge whether a person has an "apparent" purpose.
- Fair notice is required so citizens will have opportunity to conform their behavior to the law.

Concurrence (O'Connor, Breyer, JJ.). There are reasonable alternatives available to this vague ordinance. "Loiter" could be more narrowly construed.

B. STATUTORY INTERPRETATION

1. **Introduction.** Statutory interpretation issues arise frequently in the area of criminal law. Often, a defendant's freedom depends on the definition of a single word or phrase.

2. **Definition of Terms--**

United States v. Foster, 133 F.3d 704 (9th Cir. 1998).

Facts. Foster (D) and Ward manufactured methamphetamine. In time, the police "got wise to them," pulled D over when he was driving his truck, and arrested him. In a zipped-up bag under a snap-down tarp in D's truck bed, the police found a loaded semiautomatic gun and a bucket containing a scale, plastic baggies, and handwritten notes with prices. D was convicted of possessing methamphetamine and of carrying a firearm during and in relation to a drug trafficking crime in violation of federal law. D appeals, arguing in part that he was not "carrying" a firearm for purposes of the law.

Issue. Was D carrying a firearm for purposes of a statute prohibiting the use or carrying of a firearm while committing a drug trafficking crime?

Held. No. Judgment reversed on the count of carrying a firearm.

- ♦ While the word "carry" can mean simply to transport, this court has more recently held that "carry" for purposes of this statute requires that the firearm be transported on or about his person, immediately available for his use. *Black's Law Dictionary* separately defines to "carry arms or weapons" in a similar manner. Also, while the United States Supreme Court has not addressed what constitutes carrying a firearm under the statute, it narrowly defined the word "use" for the purposes of the statute as "active employment." Additionally, the Court noted that the word "use" defined broadly would become synonymous with the word "possess," a word Congress has used elsewhere but did not use in this provision. Similarly, then, a broad reading of "carry" makes it synonymous with "transport," a word Congress uses in many other places in the gun statutes, and could have used in this statute, but did not.

- ♦ Legislative history reveals that the provision was enacted to further punish violent criminals and to deter the use of guns. An offender who has ready access to a firearm is more likely to hurt someone or provoke violence. A gun in a bag under a tarp in a truck bed poses substantially less risk.

Dissent. In ordinary usage, the word "carry" includes transporting or causing to be transported. Narrowing the definition of the word for purposes of this statute is irrational. Suppose the officer had asked D to step to the rear of the vehicle while he checked his license. Would D then be carrying the gun because he now has ready access to it? What if he unzipped the bag to retrieve his license for the officer while continuing to keep the gun hidden? The majority's reasoning is too narrow. It does not work on the streets of America, which is what Congress had in mind when it drafted this statute.

IV. ACTUS REUS

A. VOLUNTARY ACT

1. **Introduction.** There are two basic elements of every crime: (i) the actus reus, or the commission of some act prohibited by law (or the omission of a legally required act); and (ii) the mens rea, or some criminal state of mind. To constitute a crime, the act must concur with intent; *i.e.,* the intent must accompany the doing of the act, and the actus reus must be attributable to the mens rea.

2. **Definition of "Act."** Some wrongful outward act or manifestation is required. Furthermore, an "act" is any event that is subject to the control of the will (although the will need not actually be exercised, since omissions to act are also punishable). Thus, to meditate is an act, but to dream is not. In all instances the "act" must be prohibited in order for a crime to exist. A person might intend to commit a crime by performing some act, but if that act is not prohibited, then there is no crime.

3. **All Acts Constituting Crime Must Be Voluntary--**

Martin v. State, 17 So. 2d 427 (Ala. 1944).

Facts. Martin (D) was arrested at his home and taken by police onto a public highway, where he used loud and profane language and manifested a drunken condition with other persons present. He was convicted of drunkenness in a public place under a state statute.

Issue. May a person be guilty of a crime if one of the acts constituting the crime was involuntarily induced?

Held. No. Conviction reversed.

- The statute presupposes that the defendant voluntarily appears in public in a drunken condition. D was brought to the public place involuntarily by the arresting officers. Thus, although he was intoxicated, the state cannot establish that he voluntarily appeared in public in that condition.

4. **"Conditioned Response" or Unconsciousness--**

State v. Utter, 479 P.2d 946 (Wash. 1971).

Facts. Utter (D), a combat veteran, and his son lived together. The son entered the apartment, said, "Dad, don't," and then stumbled into the hallway of the apartment building and collapsed, having been stabbed in the chest. He stated, "Dad stabbed me," and died before he could be questioned further. At trial, D testified that on the date in question, he had drunk a considerable amount of alcohol and had no recollection of the incident. He also offered the testimony of a psychiatrist as to "conditioned response," "an act or pattern of activity occurring so rapidly, so uniformly as to be automatic in response to a certain stimulus." D testified that, in two past incidents, he had reacted violently to people unexpectedly approaching him from the rear due to his jungle warfare training and experiences in World War II. The trial court ruled that conditioned response is not a defense under state law. D, charged with second degree murder, was convicted of manslaughter. D appeals.

Issue. Was it error for the trial court to instruct the jury to disregard the evidence on "conditioned response"?

Held. No.

- The question here is not of mental incapacity. Instead, it is whether a person who was automatistic, *i.e.*, not conscious of what he was doing, or unconscious at the time of the killing, is capable of committing a homicidal act for purposes of homicide law. Both the crimes of second degree murder and of manslaughter require the existence of a voluntary act.

- While D's theory has merit, it is also true that unconsciousness does not always provide a defense to a crime. A state of unconsciousness voluntarily induced through the use of drugs or alcohol, for example, cannot constitute a complete defense. If the defendant's theory is presented to the jury in a case such as this one, the jury should be given a cautionary instruction with respect to voluntarily induced unconsciousness.

- D's theory should have been presented to the jury if it was supported by substantial evidence. It appears, however, that there is insufficient evidence, as there is no evidence from which the jury could determine or reasonably infer what happened in the room at the time of the stabbing.

Comment. The *Utter* court explained that while the concepts of a "voluntary act" and "mens rea" are similar, as they both point to a mental state, proof of the existence of a "voluntary act" is actually the minimal mental element necessary to establish the actus reus.

---

5. **Involuntary Acts.** The act that is the subject of a crime must be "voluntary." Thus, reflexes, convulsions, and other acts done while sleepwalking or while in the middle of an epileptic fit, etc., are not voluntary acts. In *People v. Decina,* 138 N.E.2d 799 (N.Y. 1956), Decina, aware of his epileptic condition and the likelihood of being rendered unconscious as the result of a seizure, drove his

vehicle on a public way. He suffered an attack and the car went up onto the sidewalk, killing four people. He was charged with criminal negligence in the operation of a vehicle. The court found that his actions constituted criminal negligence because he deliberately chose to take a chance by driving alone, although he was aware of his vulnerability to seizures, and did so in disregard of the results that might follow. Note the necessity of prior knowledge; a disabling attack, without any prior knowledge, would be viewed differently.

B. OMISSIONS ("NEGATIVE ACTS")

1. **General Principles.** A defendant may be criminally liable for an omission or forbearance to act when there is a legal duty for him to so act. A punishable negative act is a nonoccurrence involving a breach of defendant's legal duty to take positive action.

   a. **No legal duty to render aid--**

People v. Beardsley, 113 N.W. 1128 (Mich. 1907).

Facts. Beardsley (D) invited Blanche Burns to his home while his wife was out of town. D and Burns spent the next several days drinking. While at D's home, Burns obtained six morphine tablets. She took one and drank a beer. When D discovered the morphine, he threw the tablets on the floor and tried to crush them with his foot. Burns grabbed two or three more tablets from the floor and swallowed them. Later, Burns became unresponsive, and D asked a friend to take her to a room in the basement of the dwelling that was occupied by a man named Skoba, because D's wife would be home soon. D told Skoba to look after Burns and to let her out the back door when she woke up. Sometime that evening, Skoba became concerned about the woman's condition and called a doctor. The doctor discovered that Burns was dead, and D was convicted of manslaughter on the ground that he had a duty to care for Burns in her altered condition.

Issue. Did D have a legal duty to care for Burns?

Held. No. Judgment reversed and conviction set aside.

- There are situations in which the omission of a duty that results in the death of an individual will make the individual owing the duty guilty of manslaughter. However, the duty owed must be a legal duty, not merely a moral obligation. We therefore must determine whether D, knowing Burns's life was in danger, owed her a duty to make all reasonable efforts to save her.

- The prosecutor argues that D stood as Burns's natural guardian and protector and, as such, he owed her a legal duty, which he failed to perform. We disagree. The fact that Burns was in D's home did not create a legal duty such as is due from a husband toward his wife. D assumed no care or control over Burns. Burns was a thirty-year-old woman accustomed to visiting saloons and to the use of intoxicants. She voluntarily accompanied D to his home and voluntarily consumed alcohol and morphine. There is no evidence that D practiced any duress, fraud, or deceit upon her.

---

b. **Reporting crimes.** Generally, an individual has no duty to report a crime committed or about to be committed by another. Under federal law and the laws of many states, active concealment of a felony constitutes a crime, but mere nondisclosure does not.

c. **Knowledge.** In general, no criminal act can be found ***unless*** the defendant is shown to have had knowledge of his legal duty to act.

1) **Exceptions:**

a) Where the duty to act arises from a statute.

b) Where negligence results in the imposition of criminal liability in exceptional cases where the potential risk of harm is very great. (For example, a railroad switchman was held criminally liable for failure to throw a switch, even though his attention was distracted and he was unaware of the danger.)

2. Distinguishing Acts from Omissions--

Barber v. Superior Court, 147 Cal. App. 3d 1006 (1983).

Facts. Herbert underwent surgery at the hands of Nejdl and Barber (Ds), a surgeon and an internist. After the successful operation, Herbert suffered cardio-respiratory arrest and was placed on life-support equipment. Herbert lapsed into a coma from which he was not expected to recover. The family asked that the equipment be removed, and Ds complied with the request. Herbert continued breathing, but had to be fed intravenously. After again consulting with the family, Ds removed the intravenous tubes, and Herbert died a short while later. Ds were charged with murder, but the magistrate dismissed the complaint. The superior court ordered the magistrate to reinstate the complaint, and Ds appeal.

Issue. May the doctors be charged with murder for failure to continue to provide life-sustaining treatment?

Held. No. Judgment reversed.

- Historically, death consisted of the cessation of heart and respiratory function. Now, by statute, death consists of irreversible cessation of all brain function. By either definition, Herbert was not dead when Ds ceased further treatment.

- Disconnecting mechanical life-support devices, including the IV tubes, is comparable to withholding manually administered injection or medication. Ds could have been found criminally liable only if they had a legal duty to continue to provide life-sustaining treatment. Under these circumstances, after coordinating with Herbert's wife and children, Ds had no duty to continue treatment.

C. SOCIAL HARM

Generally, there are two types of crimes, "result crimes" and "conduct crimes." "Result crimes" are actions punished because of their unwanted outcome, *e.g.*, death. "Conduct crimes," on the other hand, are actions punished because of the specific, dangerous conduct involved, *e.g.*, driving while intoxicated. Result crimes clearly result in "social harm," as their outcomes are suffered not only by the direct victim but by society, *e.g.*, losing a sense of security. In some respects, it appears that conduct crimes involve no social harm, as such acts are punished for the purpose of avoiding and deterring social harm. In another sense, however, they do involve social harm, as the conduct punished puts society in danger.

V. MENS REA

A. NATURE OF "MENS REA"

1. **Definition.** Mens rea is a guilty or wrongful purpose, a criminal intent. The intent required is ***not*** the same for all crimes (for example, negligence may be sufficient for some crimes).

2. **A Fundamental Principle.** For hundreds of years, western nations have followed the mens rea principle to determine the propriety of charging an individual with a crime and the penalty for the crime. In *United States v. Cordoba-Hincapie*, 825 F. Supp. 485 (E.D.N.Y. 1993), Judge Weinstein stated that the evolution of this important principle has been "a continuing process of self-civilization."

3. **Motive Distinguished.** Proof of motive is immaterial in establishing criminal liability. Motives create an intent to act, while intent itself is merely a determination to act in a certain way. An accused's motive may be relevant in proving the probability of his having committed the offense and/or of having had a certain type of intent when an act was committed, but failure to prove motive will not prevent a conviction.

4. **Unforeseen Result--**

Regina v. Cunningham, 2 Q.B. 396 (1957).

Facts. Cunningham (D) tore the gas meter from the wall in a house in order to steal the money contained in the meter. He did not turn off the gas, and it leaked into the next house and partially asphyxiated D's prospective mother-in-law. D was convicted under a statute for "maliciously" causing another to take a noxious thing. D appeals.

Issue. May a person be convicted under a statute that requires malicious intent when he did not actually intend to do the harm done and did not foresee the result?

Held. No. Conviction quashed.

- "Maliciously" requires that the defendant act recklessly with foresight of the actual consequence, or it requires actual intent to do the particular harm done. Recklessness is where the defendant foresees that such harm might occur but does the act anyway.

- Malice does not require that ill will toward the person injured be shown, nor does it require that the act done in itself be unlawful (as the stealing of the gas meter was here).

- The trial judge incorrectly instructed the jury that "malicious" means wicked—doing something one knows he should not do. The jury should have been left to decide whether D foresaw possible injury occurring from his act.

B. GENERAL ISSUES IN PROVING CULPABILITY

1. Intent.

a. Types of intent

1) **Introduction.** Each crime has its own standard as to the nature and quality of the intent required. At common law there were three types of mens rea: general mens rea, specific mens rea, and criminal negligence.

2) **General intent.** General intent requires only that the accused meant to do the act he committed (*i.e.,* the prohibited result was substantially certain to flow from the intentional conduct, even if the result that occurred was not subjectively intended). For example, if A voluntarily fires a gun into the middle of a crowd, even if he does not want to injure someone, and B is killed by the gunshot, A may be held for murder (*i.e.,* he intended to fire the gun into the crowd, and objectively speaking, the killing of a person was substantially certain to follow).

   a) **Proof of general intent.** Intent is inferred by the results that occur. Therefore, general intent may be proved simply by showing that the prohibited result was caused by a voluntary act of the defendant.

   b) **Transferred intent.** When a person has the required intent to commit one criminal act, he may be held responsible for results that he did not intend if he inflicts the kind of harm intended and if the injuries sustained do not require a different mens rea.

      (1) Usually the intent from the first crime will only be transferred to the second where the first act was "malum in se." For example, if A attempts to hit B and unintentionally hits and injures C, A is guilty of assault on C.

      (2) The transfer generally occurs only where the unintended result involves the same mens rea requirement as the intended act. Therefore, if A shoots at B, misses, and the bullet strikes an oil lamp, igniting a fire, A is not

guilty of arson because arson requires that specific intent to start a fire be shown (specific intent is discussed below), and here A can only be held to have had the intent to do personal injury.

3) **Malice.** Malice can refer to a specific criminal state of mind where the defendant is subjectively cognizant of the likely harmful results of his actions, yet inexcusably carries out these potentially harmful acts. Malice may also be inferred where the defendant acts recklessly or with wanton disregard for the consequences of his actions. Finally, malice may be used in its dictionary meaning, as in the crime of malicious mischief (*i.e.*, the defendant acting out of resentment or hatred of the owner of the injured property).

4) **Acting willfully.** This term usually requires only a general mens rea but may be elevated to a standard of specific intent if expressly required by the terms of a statute.

5) **Wanton or reckless conduct.** This type of conduct consists of the intentional failure to take reasonable care when confronting a known risk. Such a failure may be subjective (*i.e.,* the defendant having been actually aware of the probable consequences of his actions) or objective (*i.e.*, a reasonable person would have known of the risk).

6) **Criminal negligence.** Criminal negligence is a flagrant and reckless disregard for the safety of others. The test applied, whether it is an act of omission or commission, is what a reasonable person would do under like circumstances.

a) **Degree of negligence required.** The lack of due care required for criminal liability is greater than that required for tort liability. How much greater is not always certain because both are supposedly measured by the same standard.

(1) **Recklessness.** The defendant acted with conscious disregard of a substantial and unjustifiable risk to another.

(2) **Criminal negligence.** The defendant failed to perceive a substantial and unjustifiable risk to another resulting from his conduct in contravention of the standard of care of the reasonable person.

b. **Intent to cause permanent disability--**

People v. Conley, 543 N.E.2d 138 (Ill. App. Ct. 1989).

Facts. Conley (D) was convicted of aggravated battery following a fight. D, in an attempt to strike the victim's friend, struck the victim in the face with a bottle, causing a permanent disability to the victim's mouth. D contends that the state failed prove beyond a reasonable doubt that he intended to cause a permanent disability. D appeals.

Issue. If a person intentionally strikes another person, may he be convicted of aggravated battery based on permanent disability if it is not proven that he intended to inflict a permanent disability?

Held. Yes. Judgment affirmed.

- A person who, in committing a battery, intentionally or knowingly causes great bodily harm or permanent disability or disfigurement, commits aggravated battery.
- It is not necessary that the defendant intended to bring about the particular injuries that resulted; it is enough that the state proves that the defendant intentionally struck the victim.
- The state has the burden of proving beyond a reasonable doubt that D had either had a "conscious objective" to achieve the harm defined or that D was "consciously aware" that the harm defined was "practically certain to be caused by his conduct."
- Problems of proof are alleviated by the presumption that one intends the natural and probable consequence of his actions.
- Intent can be inferred from the surrounding circumstances, the offender's words, the weapon used, and the force of the blow.

Comment. D also argued on appeal that the state had failed to prove beyond a reasonable doubt that the victim incurred a permanent disability. The court stated that for an injury to be deemed disabling, all that must be shown is that the victim is no longer whole such that the injured body part no longer serves the body in the same way as it did before the injury.

---

2. **The Model Penal Code Approach.** Many states have adopted the approach to mens rea found in section 2.02 of the Model Penal Code, "General Requirements of Culpability." Section 2.02 provides clarity to the mental state requirements of crimes and replaces the many common law and statutory terms with four distinct levels of culpability: purposely, knowingly, recklessly, and negligently.

    a. **American Law Institute, Model Penal Code and Commentaries, Comment to section 2.02.**

1) **Objective.** This section expresses the Code's basic requirement that unless some element of mental culpability is proved with respect to each material element of the offense, no valid criminal conviction may be obtained. This is subordinated only to the provision of section 2.05 for a narrow class of strict liability offenses.

   One of the four levels of culpability must be proved with respect to each "material element." These may involve: (i) the nature of the forbidden conduct, (ii) the attendant circumstances, and (iii) the result of the conduct. The question of which level of culpability suffices to establish liability must be addressed separately with respect to each material element.

2) **Purpose and knowledge.** The Code draws a narrow distinction between acting purposefully and knowingly. Knowledge that the requisite external circumstances exist is a common element in both concepts. But action is not purposive with respect to the nature or result of the actor's conduct unless it was his conscious object to perform an action of that nature or to cause such a result.

3) **Recklessness.** As the Code uses the term, recklessness involves conscious risk creation. It resembles acting knowingly in that a state of awareness is involved, but it is an awareness of risk that is of a probability less than substantial certainty; the matter is contingent from the actor's point of view. The risk which the actor is aware must be substantial in order for the recklessness judgment to be made. The risk must also be unjustifiable. The point is that the jury must evaluate the actor's conduct and determine whether he should be condemned. Was the behavior a gross deviation from the standard of conduct that a law-abiding person in the actor's situation would observe?

4) **Negligence.** This level of culpability does not involve a state of awareness. A person acts negligently when he inadvertently creates a substantial and unjustifiable risk of which he ought to be aware. He is liable if, given the degree and nature of the risk, his failure to perceive it is a gross deviation from the care that would be exercised by a reasonable person in his situation.

5) **Offense silent as to culpability.** Unless the kind of culpability sufficient to establish a material element of an offense has been proscribed by law, it is established if a person acted purposefully, knowingly, or recklessly. Since negligence is an exceptional basis of liability, it should be excluded as a basis unless explicitly prescribed.

3. Knowledge of Attendant Circumstances (the "Willful Blindness" Problem)--

State v. Nations, 676 S.W.2d 282 (Mo. Ct. App. 1984).

Facts. Nations (D) hired a 16-year-old girl to dance for tips at D's Main Street Disco. D was charged with endangering the welfare of a child under the age of 17. D appeals, arguing that the state failed to show that she knew the child was under 17 and therefore failed to show that she had the requisite intent under the statute to endanger a child.

Issue. Is it necessary to show that D had actual knowledge of the girl's age?

Held. Yes. Judgment reversed.

- A person commits the crime of endangering a child if he "knowingly" encourages, aids, or causes a child to engage in any conduct tending to injure the child's welfare. "Knowingly" is defined as "actual knowledge" by the statute in question.
- D claims that the girl told her she was 18 and provided identification that supported her age. In fact, the girl had no identification and never showed any to D. D was untruthful and did not know, or refused to learn, the child's age. However, this is simply recklessness, not proof of knowledge.
- The state's burden was to show that the D acted knowingly, not just recklessly.

Comment: Under the Model Penal Code, the definition of "knowledge" has been expanded so that "when knowledge of the existence of a particular fact is an element of an offense, such knowledge is established if a person is aware of a high probability of its existence." This definition of knowledge encompasses willful blindness of a fact.

4. Problems in Statutory Interpretation--

United States v. Morris, 928 F.2d 504 (2d Cir. 1991).

Facts. As a computer science student at Cornell University, Morris (D) had a computer account with explicit authorization to use computers at Cornell. Morris developed a computer worm, the goal of which was to demonstrate the inadequacies of current security systems on computer networks. D released the worm into the Internet. It was programmed to spread widely, to occupy little computer operation time, not to interfere with normal computer usage, and not to replicate itself more than once onto any one computer. D incorrectly estimated the worm's ability to replicate on a given computer. Extensive replication resulted in many machines at locations around the country either crashing or becoming "catatonic." Damage was estimated to be from $200 to $53,000 per location. D was convicted of a computer crime under the Computer Fraud and Abuse Act of 1986. The statute punishes anyone who intentionally accesses, without authorization, a "federal interest" computer and damages or prevents authorized use of information, causing damage in excess of $1,000. D appeals on the grounds that the government did not prove that he intended to prevent authorized use of the computers that were damaged.

Issue. Must the government prove not only that D intended to access the computers, but also that he intended to prevent authorized use of the computers and thereby cause loss?

Held. No. Judgment affirmed.

- The district court concluded that the intent requirement applied only to the accessing portion of the statute and not to the damages portion.
- Upon review of the statutory record, the court noted that the scienter requirement in the statute was changed from knowingly to intentionally.
- The use of a stricter mens rea standard is intended to make sure that inadvertent computer access was not proscribed by the statute. Congress sought to proscribe only intentional unauthorized access, not "mistaken, inadvertent or careless" acts of unauthorized use.
- The rationale for the mens rea requirement suggests that it modifies only the "accesses" phrase, not the "damages" phrase.
- While other statutes have maintained "dual intent" language, the decision to state the scienter requirement only once, along with the decision to change it from knowingly to intentionally, evinces a clear intent on the part of Congress to modify only the "accesses" phrase.

C. STRICT LIABILITY OFFENSES

1. **Introduction.** Strict liability criminal statutes have been adopted to deal with particular problems for which the mens rea requirement was ineffective. These statutes have distinct characteristics.

2. **Public Welfare Offenses.** In *United States v. Cordoba-Hincapie* (*supra* at A.2.), the court noted the exception to the mens rea principle in public welfare offenses. Criminal liability may be found without regard to fault when these offenses involve a relatively small fine and do not include imprisonment, such as with minor traffic violations.

3. Interpreting Mental State Requirement--

Staples v. United States, 511 U.S. 600 (1994).

Facts. Staples (D) was convicted under the National Firearms Act of possessing a firearm that was not properly registered. While executing a search warrant, agents of the Bureau of Alcohol, Tobacco and Firearms (BATF) confiscated an AR-15 rifle from D's home. The AR-15 is a semi-automatic rifle, which can be modified to be an automatic weapon. The National Firearms Act requires all automatic weapons to be registered. The BATF agents claimed that D's weapon had modifications that allowed it to fire as an automatic weapon and, when tested, the weapon fired more than one shot with a single pull of the trigger. D argued that he was ignorant of any automatic firing capability and therefore is exempt from criminal liability for failing to register the gun. He requested that the jury be instructed that the government must prove beyond a reasonable doubt that he knew that the gun would fire fully automatically. The district court denied D's request, and the court of appeals affirmed. The Supreme court granted certiorari.

Issue. Must the government prove beyond a reasonable doubt that D knew that his weapon was fully automatic and therefore needed to be registered?

Held. Yes. Judgment reversed and case remanded.

- To determine the mental state requirement for a federal crime, we look to the construction of the statute and infer the intent of Congress. The National Firearms Act is silent concerning a mens rea requirement. However, silence on this point does not necessarily suggest that Congress intended to dispense with a mens rea element. The existence of a mens rea element is the rule rather than the exception. The common law rule requiring mens rea has been followed in regard to statutory crimes even where the statutory definition did not include it.

- The government argues that this case falls under "public welfare" or "regulatory" law and that this case is precisely the sort of regulatory offense described in *United States v. Freed*, 401 U.S. 601 (1971). However, our previous analysis in *Freed* was premised on the assumption that the defendant knew that he possessed particularly dangerous items (hand granades). That assumption is not warranted here.

- The harsh penalty attached to the violation of the Act—up to 10 years imprisonment—is another factor tending to suggest that Congress did not intend to eliminate a mens rea requirement. Thus, the usual presmption that a defendant must know of the illegality of his conduct should apply.

- This holding is a narrow one and depends critically on our view that if Congress had intended to make outlaws of gun owners who were wholly ignorant of the offending characteristics of their weapons and subject them to lengthy prison terms, it would have spoken clearly to that effect.

Dissent (Stevens, Blackmun, JJ.). The Court is preoccupied with guns "that can be owned with perfect innocence." This case involves a semi-automatic weapon that can be readily converted into a machine gun. This is particularly dangerous, and, in fact a substantial percent of the unregistered machine guns in circulation are converted semi-automatic weapons. The text of this statute provides explicit guidance in this case. It contains no knowledge requirements, nor does it describe a common law crime. Because this offense is entirely the creature of statute, the "background rules of common law" do not apply. Although the lack of an express knowledge requirement is not dispositive, its absence suggests that Congress did not intend to require proof that the defendant knew all the facts that made his conduct illegal. The National Firearms Act is unquestionably a public welfare statute.

---

4. Statutory Rape and Mistake-of-Age Defense --

Garnett v. State, 632 A.2d 797 (Md. 1993).

Facts. Garnett (D), a retarded man with an I.Q. of 52, was 20 years old when he engaged in "consensual" sexual intercourse with a 13-year-old girl. D was tried for second degree rape under Maryland's statutory rape law, prohibiting sexual intercourse with a person who is under 14 years of age. The defense offered evidence that the victim and her friends had told D that the victim was 16 years old and that D had acted with that belief on the night in question. The trial court excluded this evidence on the ground that even a good faith mistake as to the age of the victim was no defense. D was convicted, and he appeals.

Issues.

(i) Does Maryland's statutory rape law contain an element of mens rea?

(ii) Does Maryland's statutory rape law permit a defense of reasonable mistake of age?

Held. (i) No. (ii) No. Judgment affirmed.

- The language and legislative history of the statute do not indicate a mens rea requirement nor a mistake-of-age defense.

Dissent. The state must still prove D's intent or knowledge, which D can defend with evidence of mistake of fact. The majority holding is inconsistent with due process.

D. MISTAKE AND MENS REA

1. **Introduction.** Mistake of fact or of law is a defense to a crime that requires specific intent; a mistaken person simply lacks the specific intent required. For example, a person who takes the property of another would not be guilty of theft if he believed that the property was his own. The jury will decide what the accused actually believed. As to general intent crimes, mistake of law is not a defense. Mistake of fact may be a defense if the mistake is reasonable and the accused's actions would have been lawful had the facts been as he believed.

2. **Mistake of Fact--**

People v. Navarro, 160 Cal. Rptr. 692 (Cal. App. Dep't Super Ct. 1979)

Facts. Navarro (D) was convicted of petty theft under the California Penal Code for taking wooden beams from a construction site. D argued that he believed that the beams were abandoned. The trial court refused to use D's proposed jury instructions that allowed for acquittal even if D's good faith belief that the property was abandoned was unreasonable. Instead, the court instructed the jury that "if one takes personal property in the reasonable and good faith belief that it has been abandoned or discarded by the true owner, he is not guilty of theft . . . . If you have a reasonable doubt that the defendant had the required criminal intent as specified in these instructions, the defendant is entitled to an acquittal." D appeals on the grounds that the jury was improperly instructed.

Issue. Must a defendant's good faith belief that property was abandoned be reasonable for the defendant to be acquitted of petty theft?

Held. No. Judgment reversed.

- The statute in question codified the common law definition of larceny as the trespassory taking and carrying away of the personal property of another with the intent to steal the property.
- Because of the requirement of a specific intent to steal, there is no such thing as larceny by negligence.
- An honest mistake of fact or law is a defense when it negates a required mental element of a crime.
- The trial court erred in instructing the jury that D's good faith belief that the beams were abandoned needed to be reasonable.
- The jury could conclude that D had a good faith belief that the beams were abandoned, and even though such belief was unreasonable as measured by the

objective standard of a hypothetical reasonable man, D was entitled to acquittal since the specific intent required to be proved as an element had not been established.

Comment. At common law, a reasonable mistake of fact, but not an unreasonable one, ordinarily exculpates a defendant prosecuted for a general intent crime.

---

3. **Mistake (or Ignorance) of Law.** Mistake or ignorance of law arises in two entirely different contexts: (i) those in which, because of ignorance or mistake as to a collateral law, the defendant lacked the mental state required for a conviction; and (ii) those in which the defendant had the requisite mental state but claims that he was unaware that his conduct was proscribed by the criminal law.

   a. **Mistake as to collateral law.** Some crimes involve a particular belief concerning a legal matter. If the defendant was ignorant or mistaken as to that legal matter, he lacked the necessary mens rea. This is a mistake not regarding the criminal statute itself, but a collateral law. For example, if a person mistakenly believes that he owns certain property that he finds, when in fact he does not, he could not be convicted of larceny if he keeps the property.

   b. **Mistake as to criminal statute.** Criminal mens rea requires only that the defendant intended to do the prohibited act. Ignorance or mistake of the law is not a defense, on the theory that such a defense would undermine the enforcement of laws. The rule encourages the public to learn the laws. There are exceptions, however.

      1) **Statute later held unconstitutional.** A defendant who acted in good faith reliance upon a statute that permitted her conduct may assert this reliance as a defense, even though the statute was later invalidated.

      2) **Judicial decision.** If a judicial decision held that the particular conduct was not criminal, a defendant who relied on the decision may assert that reliance as a defense. In most jurisdictions, the decision does not need to be that of the highest state court.

      3) **Official interpretation.** Reliance upon an official interpretation of the law by one responsible for administering or enforcing the law may constitute a defense.

      4) **Advice of private counsel not a defense.** Unlike the exceptions set forth above, the courts have held that a person who in good

faith relies on the advice of private counsel may not assert that reliance as a defense.

c. **Statutory interpretation—general intent crime--**

People v. Marrero, 507 N.E.2d 1068 (N.Y. 1987).

Facts. Marrero (D) was a federal corrections officer. D carried a loaded .38 caliber automatic pistol, but he was not licensed to do so. He was arrested for violating the unlicensed possession law. By its terms, the law did not apply to "peace officers," which was defined to include corrections officers of any penal correctional institution. D claimed that he was exempt from the law because of his status, but he was charged with the violation. The trial court dismissed the indictment, but the appellate court reversed and reinstated the indictment. At his trial, D requested a jury instruction that would have led to an acquittal if the jury found that he reasonably believed the exemption applied to him. The court refused the instruction, and the appellate court affirmed. D appeals.

Issue. Is a misinterpretation of a statute a valid defense to a crime if specific intent is not an element of the crime?

Held. No. Judgment affirmed.

- When specific intent is an element of the crime, a mistake of law may constitute a defense. In a kidnapping, for example, if the defendant believed that he seized the victim with authority of law, he could not have the necessary intent to confine another without authority of law. In this case, however, liability for weapons possession is imposed regardless of the defendant's intent, so a mistake of law is no defense.

- The mistake of law defense applies when the defendant has relied on an official statement of the law contained in a statute or an official interpretation of the statute. D claims that his reasonable but mistaken interpretation of the statute should constitute a defense. However, the proper rule is that the defense applies when the defendant relies on an official statement of the law that is thereafter determined to be invalid or incorrect. It applies only when the statute in fact authorizes the conduct, not when a defendant incorrectly reads the law.

- The narrow defense of mistake of law is intended to encourage respect for and adherence to the law. D's proposed approach would instead encourage mistakes about the law. Defendants could in many cases come up with reasonable but mistaken interpretations of criminal statutes that would constitute a defense.

Dissent. A person should not be convicted for committing an act that is not inherently wrong or immoral, but is a crime solely because of a statute, if the person acted in good faith but mistakenly believed that the act was not an offense because of the wording of the statute. Such a person has not knowingly committed an offense, so there is no rationale for punishment. The common law notion was formed when crimes were acts that by their nature were evil. That approach should not be carried forward to apply to conduct that would be lawful but for a criminal statute. This is the basic difference between acts malum in se and malum prohibitum. In this case, D's interpretation of the statute was certainly reasonable. The more just approach would be to permit a defense based on a defendant's good-faith but mistaken belief based on a well-grounded interpretation of an official statement of the law contained in a statute.

---

d. Statutory interpretation—specific intent crime--

Cheek v. United States, 498 U.S. 192 (1991)

Facts. Cheek (D) was convicted of a felony for willfully evading paying federal income taxes which is a specific intent crime. D filed federal income tax returns through 1979 but thereafter ceased to file returns. At trial, evidence established that D was involved in at least four civil cases that challenged various aspects of the federal income tax system. Many of the challenges were deemed frivolous and were rejected by the courts. D also testified that he attended seminars sponsored by a group believing that the federal tax system is unconstitutional. D's defense was that he believed that the tax laws were being unconstitutionally enforced and that his failure to file tax returns was lawful. D therefore argued that he had acted without the willfulness required for conviction. The trial court instructed the jury that an objectively reasonable good-faith misunderstanding of the law was a defense to willfulness, but mere disagreement with the law was not. While deliberating, the jury indicated that they were divided as to D's honest and reasonable belief that he owed no taxes. The judge gave further instructions that "an honest but unreasonable belief is not a defense and does not negate willfulness." The jury returned a guilty verdict, D appealed, and the court of appeals affirmed. The Supreme Court granted certiorari.

Issue. Must a defendant's good faith belief that the law does not apply to him be objectively reasonable for it to be a defense to a crime requiring specific intent?

Held. No. Judgment vacated and case remanded.

- We have long held that ignorance of the law is no defense. However, the proliferation of statutes and regulations has made it difficult for the average citizen to know and comprehend the extent of the duties and obligations imposed by the tax laws. Thus, Congress has made specific intent to violate the law an element of certain federal criminal tax offenses.

- In *United States v. Murdock,* 290 U.S. 389 (1933), the Court held that an accused is entitled to an instruction as to whether he acted in good faith based on his actual belief. The Court defined "willfully" as "an act done with a bad purpose" or with "an evil motive." Since then, willfulness has been described as "a voluntary, intentional violation of a known legal duty."

- ♦ Willfulness in criminal tax cases requires the government to prove that: (i) the law imposed a duty on the defendant, (ii) the defendant knew of this duty, and (iii) the defendant voluntarily and intentionally violated that duty. If D asserted that he truly believed that the Internal Revenue Code did not purport to treat wages as income, and the jury believed him, the government would not have carried their burden to prove willfulness, no matter how unreasonable a court might deem D's belief.

- ♦ We disagree with the court of appeals's requirement that a defendant's good-faith belief be objectively reasonable in order to negate the government's evidence purporting to show the defendant's awareness of the legal duty at issue. Of course, the more unreasonable the defendant's asserted beliefs are, the more likely the jury will consider them to be merely a simple disagreement with a known legal duty.

- ♦ Although the court of appeals erred in instructing the jury that a claimed good-faith belief must be objectively reasonable, it was not error to instruct the jury not to consider D's argument that the tax laws were unconstitutional.

- ♦ The *Murdock* line of cases does not support D's assertion that he should be acquitted because he believed in good faith that the income tax law is unconstitutional as applied to him and thus could not impose a duty on him. Those cases construed the willfulness requirement as requiring proof of knowledge of the law. D's claim that some of the provisions of the tax code are unconstitutional is not based on a mistake caused by the complexity of tax law. His claim reveals a full knowledge of the provisions at issue. Furthermore, D paid his taxes for years before concluding that the income tax laws could not constitutionally require him to pay a tax. Therefore, D's views about the validity of tax laws are irrelevant to the issue of willfulness and need not be heard by the jury. Nevertheless, this case is remanded because D's belief that he was not required to file a tax return or pay income taxes did not have to be objectively reasonable to be considered by the jury.

Dissent (Blackmun, Marshall, JJ.). This Court's opinion today will encourage taxpayers to cling to frivolous views of the law in the hope of convincing a jury of their sincerity.

Comment. In *Marrero,* the defendant was not permitted to raise a claim of reasonable mistake of law. In *Cheek*, the defendant was permitted to claim a patently unreasonable mistake of law. Note that *Cheek* involved a specific intent crime and *Marrero* involved a general intent crime.

VI. CAUSATION

A. ACTUAL CAUSE (CAUSE-IN-FACT)

1. **"But For" Rule.** The defendant's act must have actually caused the unlawful result before he can be held criminally liable. The defendant is the cause if, "but for" his antecedent conduct, the result would not have occurred.

   a. **Substantial factor test distinguished.** In *Velazquez v. State, infra*, the court compared the "but for" test with the "substantial factor" test. Under the traditional "but for" test, a defendant's conduct is a cause-in-fact of the prohibited result if the result would not have occurred "but for" the defendant's conduct. On the other hand, the substantial factor test is appropriate when two defendants, acting independently, commit two separate acts, each of which alone is sufficient to bring about a prohibited result. For example, if two defendants concurrently inflict mortal wounds upon another person, each of which is sufficient to cause death, each defendant's action would not be considered a "but for" cause of death because the deceased would have died even in the absence of one of the defendant's actions. However, each defendant's action in independently and concurrently inflicting mortal wounds on the deceased constitutes a "substantial factor" in bringing about the deceased's death and thus is a cause-in-fact of the death. Therefore, a defendant's conduct will sometimes be a substantial factor even though it was not a "but for" cause.

   b. **"But for" test applied--**

Oxendine v. State, 528 A.2d 870 (Del. 1987).

Facts. Oxendine (D) was convicted of manslaughter in the beating death of his six-year-old son, Jeffrey. The evidence showed that D's girlfriend, Tyree, pushed Jeffrey into a bathtub, causing microscopic tears in Jeffrey's intestines. The next morning, D beat Jeffrey for about five to 10 minutes. Later that day, Jeffrey's abdomen became swollen, and Tyree urged D to take Jeffrey to the hospital. Instead, D went out to buy a newspaper. When D returned home, Tyree had prepared to take Jeffrey to the hospital. On the way to the hospital, Jeffrey stopped breathing, and he was pronounced dead shortly after arriving at the hospital.

During trial, the medical evidence showed that had D inflicted a nonlethal injury on his son after Jeffrey had sustained an earlier, lethal injury from Tyree. However, the two medical examiners called by the state were unable to say with any degree of medical certainty whether the second injury contributed to Jeffrey's death. Furthermore, one of the doctors stated that he could not give an opinion as to whether the second injury accelerated Jeffrey's death, and the other doctor was not asked his opinion as to acceleration. Nevertheless, the state's only theory of causation was the acceleration theory, and the court instructed the jury that contribution without acceleration was not sufficient to establish causation. D moved for a judgment of acquittal, but his motion was denied. D appeals.

Issue. To convict a defendant of manslaughter under the acceleration theory of causation, must the state establish that, but for the defendant's infliction of the second injury, the victim would not have died as soon as he did?

Held. Yes. Judgment reversed and case remanded.

- ♦ For D to be convicted of manslaughter, the state had to show that D's conduct caused his son's death. Under Delaware law, causation is the "antecedent but for which the result in question would not have occurred." Thus, if the second injury caused Jeffrey to die any sooner than he otherwise would have, D would be deemed to have caused Jeffrey's death.
- ♦ A doctor's testimony can only be considered evidence if his conclusions are based on reasonable medical certainty. Here, the testimony of the medical examiners called by the state was insufficient to sustain the state's acceleration theory. Therefore, D's conviction of manslaughter must be set aside for insufficiency of evidence to establish that his conduct accelerated his son's death.
- ♦ The trial court properly denied D's motion for judgment of acquittal because the medical testimony for the state was sufficient for a rational trier of fact to conclude beyond a reasonable doubt that D was guilty of the lesser included offense of assault in the second degree.

B. PROXIMATE CAUSE ("LEGAL" CAUSE)

1. **Introduction.** Under certain circumstances, the "but for" test could impose liability on persons who are only remotely responsible for a prohibited consequence. The doctrine of proximate causation serves the purpose of determining which persons among those who satisfy the "but for" standard should be held accountable for the resulting harm. Thus, even though a person's conduct may actually cause another's death, this conduct is not necessarily the proximate or legal cause of death. A person cannot be a proximate cause of harm unless he an actual cause, but he can be an actual cause without being the proximate cause. Issues of proximate causation usually arise when there is an intervening force, such as: (i) an act of God, (ii) an act of an independent third party that accelerates or aggravates the harm caused by the defendant or that causes it to occur in an unexpected manner, or (iii) an act or omission of the victim that helps to bring about the outcome.

2. Intervening Force--

Kibbe v. Henderson, 534 F.2d 493 (2d Cir. 1976).

Facts. Kibbe (D) and Krall (D's codefendant) saw Stafford at a bar, where the bartender refused to serve Stafford another drink because he was already intoxicated. D and Krall volunteered to give Stafford a ride, intending to rob him. As Krall was driving, D robbed Stafford and forced him to lower his trousers and remove his boots to prove that he had no more money. After robbing him, D and Krall abandoned Stafford on a rural two-lane highway no more than one-quarter mile from a gas station. About half an hour later, Blake, who was driving 50 m.p.h. (10 m.p.h. over the speed limit), saw Stafford sitting on the road. Blake testified that he went into shock and did not have time to react before hitting Stafford. After the collision, Blake returned to help Stafford. Stafford was mortally injured, his trousers were around his ankles, and he had on neither his jacket nor boots. An autopsy revealed that Stafford's blood alcohol level was .25%, and the medical examiner testified that the injuries from the accident were the direct cause of death. At the trial, the judge failed to explain to the jury the issue of causation as it is used in the definition of second degree murder and did not mention the legal effect of intervening or supervening cause. D and Krall were convicted of second degree murder. D's conviction was affirmed by the appellate court on a finding that there was sufficient evidence showing that Stafford's death was caused by D's acts as well as by the acts of Blake. The district court denied a petition for habeas corpus relief. D appeals on the issue of habeas corpus relief.

Issue. Must a jury be given detailed instructions on the issue of causation if an intervening force is present in the facts?

Held. Yes. Writ granted with respect to the murder count.

- Under New York law, "A person is guilty of murder in the second degree when: . . . [u]nder circumstances evincing a depraved indifference to human life, he recklessly engages in conduct which creates a grave risk of death to another person, and thereby causes the death of another person."

- Because causation was a pivotal issue at trial, the judge's failure to instruct the jury with respect to causation allowed the jury to convict without finding that every element of the crime had been proven beyond a reasonable doubt. The jury could have concluded that the issue of causation was not before them or that causation could be inferred merely from the fact that Stafford's death succeeded his abandonment by D and Krall. Even if the jury were aware of the causation issue, they did not receive sufficient instruction on this issue.

- The legal standard in a case like this is complex. Where death is caused by an intervening force, such as the collision here, the liability of one who put an antecedent force into action depends on whether the intervening force was a sufficiently independent or supervening cause of death. The few cases with similar fact patterns suggest that the controlling issues are whether the ultimate result was foreseeable to the original actor and whether the victim failed to do something easily within his reach that would have extricated him from danger.

- The court's incomplete instructions took a necessary determination of causation of death from the jury and deprived D of due process.

Comment. After D's petition for habeas corpus was granted, the state of New York appealed. The United States Supreme Court reversed the judgment, holding that the trial court's failure to instruct the jury on causation did not so infect the trial as to violate due process. [Henderson v. Kibbe, 431 U.S. 145 (1977)]

---

3. Deceased's Own Actions Caused Death--

Velazquez v. State, 561 So. 2d 347 (Fl. 1990)

Facts. Velasquez (D) participated in an illegal drag race with Alvarez. After the race, Alvarez suddenly turned his car around and proceeded back toward the starting line, and D followed. Alvarez was not wearing a seatbelt and attained an estimated speed of 123 m.p.h. Although Alvarez had a blood alcohol level between .11 and .12, D had not been drinking. As they reached the starting line, Alvarez applied his brakes but could not stop. His car crashed through a guardrail and was propelled over a canal, landing on the far bank. Alvarez was thrown from his car, was pinned under his car when it landed on him, and died instantly. D also crashed through the guardrail, but he landed in the canal and was able to escape.

Issue. Is a defendant guilty of vehicular homicide when the sole basis for imposing liability is his participation in an illegal drag race that resulted in the death of another participant?

Held. No. Judgment reversed and case remanded.

- Even where a defendant's conduct is the cause-in-fact of a prohibited result, criminal liability should not be imposed where the prohibited result of the defendant's conduct is beyond the scope of any fair assessment of the danger created by the defendant's conduct or where it would otherwise be unjust, based on fairness and policy considerations, to hold the defendant criminally responsible for the prohibited result.

- People often join together in reckless conduct, but if all participants do so knowingly and voluntarily, there is no point in holding a survivor guilty of manslaughter if the reckless conduct results in death.

- Applying the "but for" test—but for D's participation in the drag race, the deceased would not have recklessly raced his vehicle at all. However, the issue is not whether D's reckless conduct was the cause-in-fact of the deceased's death, but whether D's conduct was the legal cause of the deceased's death.

- D's participation in the race was not the proximate cause of the deceased's death. The deceased in effect killed himself by his own volitional reckless driving. Therefore, it would be unjust to hold the defendant criminally responsible for the deceased's death.

C. CONCURRENCE OF THE ELEMENTS

1. **Crimes of Recklessness or Negligence.** In crimes of recklessness and negligence, it must be established that the reckless or negligent conduct (not just any conduct of the defendant) caused the prohibited result.

2. **Manslaughter--**

State v. Rose, 3 A.2d 281 (R.I. 1979).

Facts. Rose (D), while driving his car, struck McEnery. McEnery's body first was thrown up on the hood, then rolled off and was wedged under the car. D then drove the car several hundred feet from the scene of the accident. At trial, the testimony of the only medical witness established that McEnery could have died either at the time of the primary impact or later, while being dragged under D's car. D was convicted of manslaughter and leaving the scene of an accident. D appeals.

Issue. For a manslaughter conviction, must a defendant's negligence precede the death?

Held. Yes. The conviction is reversed.

- To be liable, D's negligence had to cause McEnery's death. There was no evidence that D was negligent up to and at the time McEnery was hit by D's car. Therefore, to find D guilty of manslaughter, it would be necessary to find that McEnery was alive immediately after impact and that D's conduct after impact constituted culpable negligence.

- Because the testimony of the medical witness lacked reasonable medical certainty as to the time of death, we are unable to conclude beyond a reasonable doubt that D was guilty of manslaughter. Thus, the trial court erred in denying D's motion for directed verdict of acquittal with respect to the charge of manslaughter, but not with respect to the charge of leaving the scene of an accident.

VII. CRIMINAL HOMICIDE

A. INTRODUCTION

Homicide is the killing of one human by another. Homicide is not necessarily a crime, but it is a material element for the crimes of murder and manslaughter.

1. **Types of Homicide.** There are three types of homicide.

   a. **Justifiable homicide.** A homicide is justifiable if it is commanded or authorized by law, such as when committed in execution of a sentence of death, in preventing an escape, or in pursuit of a dangerous fleeing felon.

   b. **Excusable homicide.** Excusable homicide may be either accidental or in self-defense.

      1) **Accidental.** For accidental homicide, the person must have committed the homicide while performing a lawful act with due care and without any intention of hurting the other.

      2) **Self-defense.** Self-defense involves killing another upon sudden affray, merely in one's own defense or in defense of one's spouse, child, or parent, and not from any vindictive feeling.

      3) **Comment.** Other homicides are excusable as a result of the status of the person committing the act (infants, feeble-minded persons, etc.), or because of an actual and reasonable mistake of fact.

   c. **Criminal homicide.** Criminal homicide is the killing of another human being without justification or excuse. The two important classifications here are "murder" and "manslaughter."

2. **Elements of Criminal Homicide.**

   a. **Corpus delicti (the body of the crime).** The corpus delicti of a criminal homicide consists of two elements:

      (i) A person is deceased; and

      (ii) The death is a result of someone's criminality.

      1) **The victim.**

         a) **Fetus.** There is controversy over whether an unborn infant was "living" at the time of the act that purportedly resulted in its death.

(1) **Majority view.** The majority view presumes a child to be dead until proven otherwise. The proof of life required is that the child be expelled from the mother and using its own circulatory system.

(2) **Minority view.** The minority view holds that the killing of a fetus is homicide.

b) **Vital signs--**

People v. Eulo, 472 N.E.2d 286 (N.Y. 1984).

Facts. In separate incidents, Eulo and Bonilla (Ds) shot a person in the head, the person was unconscious when brought to the hospital, and the person was placed on a respirator. Later, after it was determined that each victim's brain was no longer functioning, each victim was declared dead, artificial respiration was terminated, and organs were removed for transplantation. At each trial, while there was much evidence as to the victims' brain death, there was no specific instruction as to whether death, for purposes of state homicide law, occurs with brain death or with the irreversible cessation of breathing and heartbeat. The state statute does not expressly define "death." Ds were convicted of manslaughter. Ds appeal.

Issue. Does the irreversible cessation of brain activity constitute "death" for purposes of state homicide law when artificial means allow the person to breathe and his heart to beat?

Held. Yes. Judgments affirmed.

- Within a short period after being deprived of oxygen, the brain will irreversibly stop functioning. This "brain death" will end all spontaneous bodily functions. Artificial means may still maintain certain heart and breathing functions.

- After an examination of the common law conception of death and the traditional criteria used to determine when death occurs, we find that a recognition of brain-based criteria for determining death is not unfaithful to prior judicial definitions of "death." Ordinarily, death will be determined according to traditional criteria of irreversible cardiorespiratory repose. When, however, the body continues to breathe only by artificial means, death may be deemed to occur when it is determined that the entire brain's function has irreversibly ceased. This reflects an improved understanding that in the complete and irreversible absence of a functioning brain, the heart and lungs will function only as a result of artificial stimuli and will never again function as part of an integrated organism.

---

2) **Omission to act.** Where there exists a legal duty to act, an omission to so act will constitute criminal homicide if such omission results in the killing of another human being. For example, the court found a legal duty existed where two elderly women lived together and one became incapacitated. The other did nothing to help her, creating culpable negligence when the first woman died.

b. **Time limit.** At common law, the death had to occur within one year and one day after the defendant's unlawful act causing the injury or there could be no prosecution for murder. Many courts and legislatures have since concluded that the rule is "anachronistic" due to medical advances and no longer follow the rule.

c. **Criminal state of mind.** Determination of the mental element (mens rea) is usually more difficult to establish than the physical element (actus reus). The classification of the mens rea distinguishes murder from manslaughter and the various degrees thereof.

B. INTENTIONAL KILLINGS

Murder is the unlawful killing of a human being by another human being with malice aforethought. This malice may be actual or may be implied by law.

1. Degrees of Murder: The Deliberation-Premeditation Formula

a. **Malice aforethought.** The term "malice aforethought" does not approximate its literal meaning. Rather than relying on this misleading phrase, it is more appropriate to consider the various types of mens rea for murder that the common law came to recognize and that exist today in most jurisdictions:

1) **Intent to kill.** Conduct, accompanied by an intent to kill, that causes another's death constitutes murder, unless there are mitigating circumstances present or the homicide is either justifiable or excusable.

2) **Intent to inflict serious bodily harm.** Conduct coupled with an intent to do serious bodily injury but without an intent to kill, which causes another's death, constitutes murder.

3) **Depraved heart.** Reckless conduct that a reasonable person would realize creates a high degree of risk of death or serious bodily injury to another, which actually causes the death of another, may constitute murder.

b. **First and second degree murder.**

1) **Introduction.** At common law, there were no degrees of murder. All homicide with "malice aforethought" was murder and was punished by death. In order to reduce the punishment for less grievous homicides, most states classify murder. The typical classification is first degree (homicide with "premeditation") and second degree (without "premeditation") murder.

2) **First degree murder.** First degree murder is all homicide with malice aforethought that is either (i) encompassed within the felony-murder rule of the jurisdiction (usually heinous felonies), or (ii) willful, deliberate, and premeditated.

   a) **Willful.** The defendant must actually intend to kill.

   b) **Deliberate.** The defendant must be possessed of a cool mind that is capable of reflection.

   c) **Premeditated.** The defendant, having a cool mind, must in fact reflect before his act of killing. The defendant's state of mind is decisive during the length of time between the formation of the idea to kill and the actual killing.

   d) **Proof of state of mind.** Premeditation, deliberation, and willful intent are subjective states of mind. The existence of these elements must be determined from the defendant's conduct in light of the surrounding circumstances.

   e) **Presumption of premeditation for certain homicides.** Homicides perpetrated by poison or torture or after lying in wait for the victim, etc., are presumed by common law to have been premeditated.

3) **Second degree murder.** In most states, murder not falling within the first degree murder category is second degree murder.

   a) **No premeditation.** Those murders committed with the intent to kill but lacking premeditation and deliberation are of the second degree.

      (1) **Intentional.** Both first and second degree murder include "intentional" homicide. Since it may actually be impossible for the mind to function in a way so that an intentional homicide occurs without at least some premeditation, the only difference between first and second degree murder exists in the degree of the premeditation (a difficult distinction to make).

      (2) **Voluntary manslaughter.** Voluntary manslaughter is an intentional homicide committed under extenuating

circumstances that mitigate but do not justify or excuse the killing. The principal extenuating circumstance is that the defendant acted in a state of passion engendered by adequate provocation. However, if the rationale of second degree murder is that it does not involve premeditation, then a conflict between it and intentional (voluntary) manslaughter inevitably arises. Voluntary manslaughter does not include malice (since it is a homicide that arises from a sudden passion and on adequate provocation). Therefore, it seems that the difference between voluntary manslaughter and second degree murder is in the adequacy of the provocation that causes the killer's act—a more substantial provocation must be required to classify the homicide as voluntary manslaughter.

b) **Felony-murder.** Those felony-murders where the felony in question is not enumerated in the first degree murder statute are considered to be second degree murder.

c) **Wanton disregard for human life.** Killings that indicate the defendant's wanton and willful disregard for human life are also second degree murder (*e.g.*, playing "Russian roulette" with a loaded revolver).

(1) This standard seems to approach the negligence standard, but in order for second degree murder to exist, the defendant's act must be sufficiently wanton to imply malice.

(2) Involuntary manslaughter may also arise from criminal negligence (although sufficient wantonness is not present to imply malice aforethought). Here again, the distinction between second degree murder and involuntary manslaughter is a difficult one to draw.

(3) Criminal negligence, even of a wanton nature, cannot ever amount to first degree murder because negligence necessarily rules out the possibility of premeditation.

(4) The element of provocation, which is discussed *infra* in connection with manslaughter, may reduce murder to manslaughter.

(5) The character of the defendant (*e.g.*, personal turpitude) may also have an effect on whether the murder is held to be first or second degree murder.

4) **Lesser included offenses.** Typically, a defendant, upon his request, the prosecutor's request, or sometimes absent any request, has a right to have the jury instructed that he can be convicted of a lesser offense than that charged. For example, if a defendant is charged with first degree murder, the jury might be instructed that the defendant may be convicted of second degree murder if he is found to have intentionally killed a person but not in a premeditated and deliberate manner.

c. **Time required for premeditation and deliberation--**

State v. Guthrie, 461 S.E.2d 163 (W. Va. 1995).

Facts. Guthrie (D) and Farley worked together as dishwashers. On the night of the killing, Farley was poking fun at D, who was in a bad mood. Farley told D to "lighten up" and snapped him with a dishtowel. When the dishtowel hit D's nose, D became enraged, moved toward Farley, pulled a knife from his pocket, and stabbed Farley in the neck. D suffered from a variety of psychiatric problems, including daily panic attacks, chronic depression, borderline personality disorder, and an obsession with his nose (body dysmorphic disorder). At trial, D testified that he suffered a panic attack immediately before the stabbing. D was convicted of first degree murder. D appeals.

Issue. Must there be a period of time for prior consideration before a killing for there to be the premeditation and deliberation required for first degree murder?

Held. Yes. Judgment reversed and case remanded.

- The jury was instructed that murder in the first degree occurs when one person kills another person unlawfully, willfully, maliciously, deliberately, and premeditatedly. In its effort to define these terms, the trial court instructed the jury that: (i) to constitute a willful, deliberate, and premeditated killing, the intention to kill need not exist for any particular length of time before the actual killing, but must have come into existence for the first time at the time of such killing or at any time previously; (ii) to constitute a premeditated murder, an intent to kill need exist only for an instant; and (iii) what is meant by the language willful, deliberate, and premeditated is that the killing be intentional. These instructions failed to adequately inform the jury of the difference between first and second degree murder and provided no guidance as to what constitutes premeditation. Also of concern is the manner in which the instructions confused premeditation with the intent to kill.

- West Virginia has retained a distinction between first and second degree murder, and it is necessary to articulate the difference. To allow the state to prove premeditation and deliberation by only showing that the intention to kill came into existence for the first time at the time of the killing eliminates the distinction between the two degrees of murder.

- Although premeditation and deliberation are not measured by any particular period of time, there must be some period between the formation of the intent to kill and the actual killing, which indicates that the accused is fully conscious of what he intended, to support a conviction for first degree murder.

---

d. Intent to kill--

Midgett v. State, 729 S.W.2d 410 (Ark. 1987).

Facts. Midgett (D), who was six feet two inches tall and weighed 300 pounds, got drunk and beat his son as he had done on previous occasions, punching him in the stomach and on the back, and the son died. His son, eight years old, weighed only between 38 and 45 pounds. It was determined at the autopsy that he was very poorly nourished and underdeveloped. The autopsy and other evidence revealed that the son had been subject to severe physical abuse over a period of time. The autopsy also concluded that the son died as the result of a hemorrhage caused by blunt force trauma consistent with trauma caused by a human fist. A jury found D guilty of first degree murder, and D appeals.

Issue. Is intentional abuse of a child that results in the child's death sufficient to support a finding of first degree murder under state law?

Held. No. Conviction affirmed but modified to one of second degree murder.

- While terrible, the facts of this case are insufficient to establish the "premeditated and deliberated purpose of causing the death of another person" required for a first degree murder conviction in this state. The evidence only supports the conclusion that D intended not to kill his son but to abuse him further or that his intent, if it was to kill the child, was developed in a drunken, heated rage while disciplining the child. There is also no evidence that D starved his son.
- The evidence is sufficient to sustain a conviction of second degree murder, as D was shown to have caused his son's death by delivering a blow "with the purpose of causing serious physical injury."
- Other states have created laws to permit a finding beyond that of second degree murder in cases like these, but Arkansas has yet to do so.

Dissent. The degree of murder committed is for the jury to decide. The jury could easily conclude that D starved his son and repeatedly subjected him to severe physical abuse with the intent to kill him.

Comment. Shortly after the decision in *Midgett*, Arkansas law was amended to allow a finding of first degree murder in cases where "[u]nder circumstances manifesting extreme indifference to the value of human life," one "knowingly causes the death of a person fourteen (14) years of age or younger." [Ark. Code Ann. 5-10-101(a)(9) (Supp. 1995)]

---

e. Euthanasia--

State v. Forrest, 362 S.E.2d 252 (N.C. 1987).

Facts. Forrest (D) admitted his critically ill father to a hospital. The following day, the father's condition was determined to be untreatable and terminal, he was classified as "No Code," meaning that no extraordinary measures would be used to save his life, and he was moved to a more comfortable room. The next day, D went to visit his father. While a nurse's assistant was tending to his father, D said, "There is no need in doing that. He's dying." She responded, "Well, I think he's better." She noticed that D was sniffling as though crying and kept his hand in his pocket during the conversation. She went to get a nurse, who told him, "I don't think your father is as sick as you think he is." Visibly upset, D replied, "Go to hell. I've been taking care of him for years. I'll take care of him." After the nurse and assistant left the room, D told his father he loved him. His father began to cough, making a gurgling and rattling noise. D pulled a pistol out of his pocket and fired four shots point blank at his father's temple, cocking the pistol each time it fired. D threatened no one after the shooting and openly acknowledged that he had killed his father, saying, "I promised my dad I wouldn't let him suffer" and further elaborating that he had wanted to put an end to his suffering. Although D's father had been near death at the time of the shooting, the cause of death was found to be the four shots to his head. A jury found D guilty of first degree murder. D appeals.

Issue. Does the intentional killing of a dying person to prevent his suffering demonstrate the premeditation and deliberation required for a first degree murder conviction?

Held. Yes. Judgment affirmed.

- Some circumstances to be considered in determining whether a killing was with premeditation and deliberation are want of provocation, the defendant's conduct and statements before and after the killing, the defendant's threats and declarations before and during the occurrence giving rise to the killing, ill-will or previous difficulty between the parties, the dealing of lethal blows after the deceased has been felled and rendered helpless, and evidence that the killing was done in a brutal manner.

- Here, D's father did nothing to provoke D's actions when D was in the hospital room. His father lay helpless in the hospital bed while D fired four separate times, and D had to cock the pistol each time before firing. Also, D testified that he always carried a gun in his job as a truck driver, but he was not working on the day in question. Most significantly, D's statements after the killing show that he had thought about putting an end to his father's suffering.

---

2. Manslaughter: "Heat of Passion" Killings.

a. Common law principles.

The elements of heat of passion are:

(i) There must have been a reasonable provocation.

(ii) The defendant must have been in fact provoked.

(iii) A reasonable person so provoked would not have cooled off in the interval of time between the provocation and the delivery of the fatal blow.

(iv) The defendant must not in fact have cooled off during that interval.

1) **Provocation.** Under the common law reasonable person test, sufficient provocation is that which causes a reasonable person to lose his normal self-control. Although a reasonable person who has lost control over himself would not kill, his homicidal reaction to the provocation is at least understandable. The provocation defense is available only if the offender moves quickly (*i.e.*, succumbs to the provocation right away); too much delay can jeopardize the defense.

a) **Limitations--**

Girouard v. State, 583 A.2d 718 (Md. 1991).

Facts. During an argument, Girouard (D) killed his wife by stabbing her 19 times after she disparaged his sexual ability, barraged him with insults, said that she did not love him and wanted a divorce, and told him that she had filed charges to have him court martialed. D then nonfatally slit his own wrists and called the police. At trial, a psychologist testified that D had mental problems, was out of touch with his capacity to experience anger or express hostility, and had reached the limit of his ability to swallow his anger. The police found D wandering around outside, despondent and tearful. D was convicted of second degree murder and sentenced to 22 years in prison, 10 of which were suspended. D appeals.

Issue. Should the mitigating factor of provocation be limited only to the traditional circumstances of: extreme assault or battery upon a defendant, mutual combat, illegal arrest, injury or serious abuse of a close relative, or the sudden discovery of a defendant's spouse's adultery?

Held. Yes. Judgment affirmed.

- Under this state's "Rule of Provocation," murder should not be mitigated to manslaughter unless: (i) there was adequate provocation; (ii) the killing was done in the heat of passion; (iii) the killing followed the provocation before there was a reasonable opportunity for the passion to cool; and (iv) there was a causal connection between the provocation, the passion, and the fatal act. Even if we assume that the second, third, and fourth of these criteria were met in this case, we must examine whether there was adequate provocation.

- To be adequate, the provocation must be enough to inflame the passion of a reasonable man so that he acts out of passion rather than reason. The reasonableness standard is not affected by D's mental frailties.

- This state holds, as do other jurisdictions, that words alone, no matter how abusive or taunting, do not constitute provocation adequate to reduce the crime of murder to manslaughter. Thus, we cannot hold that a verbal domestic argument that ends in the death of a spouse can result in a conviction of manslaughter.

---

2) **Justification versus excuse.** It is unclear whether the defense of provocation is derived from a theory of justification or that of excuse. An act is justified if society approves of the defendant's conduct in light of the circumstances. An act is excused if society does not approve of the conduct but considers the defendant not to be morally blameworthy, *e.g.*, due to insanity. A reasonable conclusion is that provocation is a "partial justification"; *e.g.*, witnessing the unlawful conduct of adultery of one's wife makes the husband's killing of his wife "less socially undesirable." It is also reasonable to conclude, however, that the killing of one's wife is never justifiable, but that society's understanding that witnessing one's wife's infidelity might undermine one's ability to act within the confines of the law allows for a "partial excuse."

b. **The objective standard: Who is the "reasonable man"?**

1) **Characteristics of the "reasonable man."** Generally, a homicide constitutes manslaughter instead of murder if the defendant was provoked in a manner "calculated to inflame the passion of a reasonable man" or which "might render ordinary men, of fair average disposition, liable to act rashly or without due deliberation or reflection, and from passion, rather than judgment." Originally,

English courts held the "reasonable man" to be a figure without any of the defendant's specific characteristics. [*See* Bedder v. Director of Public Prosecutions, [1954] 2 All. Eng. Rep. 801] More recent cases take into consideration certain relevant characteristics.

2) **Chronic alcoholism--**

Attorney General for Jersey v. Holley, 3 All ER 371 (Privy Council 2005).

Facts. The defendant (D) and his live-in girlfriend, Cherylinn Mullane, were both alcoholics. Their relationship was stormy, and they often had violent arguments. After one such argument in a bar, D went home and spent the afternoon drinking and chopping wood with an axe. According to D, when Mullane returned home that evening, she was drunk and told D that she had just had sex with another man. D picked up the axe, intending to leave, when Mullane said, "You haven't got the guts." D lifted the axe and struck Mullane seven or eight times, killing her. D admitted to the killing but pled not guilty to the charge of murder, based on the defense of provocation. He was convicted of murder. This conviction was later set aside, but he was reconvicted at a retrial. D again appealed, and the court of appeal set aside the murder conviction and entered a verdict of manslaughter instead.

Issue. Should the jury have considered evidence that D was suffering from chronic alcoholism when considering whether a person having ordinary powers of self-control would have done what D did under the circumstances presented?

Held. No. But the order of the court of appeal should stand on other procedural grounds.

- This case requires examination and clarification of the law relating to provocation as a partial defense to a charge of murder. The common law recognized that, sometimes, extenuating circumstances require that a conviction of murder be reduced to the lesser offense of manslaughter.

- The defense of provocation has two ingredients. First, the subjective or factual ingredient is that the defendant was provoked into losing his self-control. This includes evidence of any mental or other abnormality making it more or less likely that the defendant lost his self-control. D's alcoholism is properly considered here.

- The second ingredient, the objective or evaluative ingredient, raises the question of whether the provocation was enough to make a reasonable person act as the defendant did. Prior cases have indicated that this standard is flexible and that the jury should apply the standard of control to be expected of the particular defendant. However, this is a departure from the law as declared by Parliament in the Homicide Act. The statute clearly states that the sufficiency of the provocation is to be judged by one standard—the "ordinary person" standard. The statute does not leave each jury free to set whatever standard it considers appropriate in the circumstances. It is not open for judges to change this standard.

- Contrary to the view of the court of appeal, evidence of D's alcoholism was not a matter to be taken into account by the jury when weighing the second ingredient and determining whether an ordinary person would have acted as D did. Thus, ordinarily the order of the court of appeal should be set aside and D's conviction for murder reinstated. But, based on certain procedural oddities in this case, the order should stand.

---

c. Model Penal Code--

People v. Casassa, 404 N.E.2d 1310 (N.Y. 1980).

Facts. Casassa (D) became infatuated with Lo Consolo, who rejected D's advances. On several occasions, D broke into the apartment below Lo Consolo's to eavesdrop on her. He also broke into Lo Consolo's apartment once when she was out. He did not take anything, but he disrobed and lay in her bed for a while. Finally, D took several bottles of liquor to Lo Consolo's apartment as a gift, but she rejected his offer. D then stabbed her to death. D eventually confessed and was charged with second degree murder. D claimed as a defense that he acted under the influence of extreme emotional disturbance based on his obsession with Lo Consolo. A state witness testified that D's mental state was the result of stress that he created within himself. The trial court considered the reasonableness of D's reaction to the events preceding the crime and concluded that the reasonableness should not be considered solely from D's point of view. The court then found that D's emotional reaction at the time of the killing was so peculiar to him that it could not be considered reasonable so as to reduce the conviction to manslaughter. D appeals.

Issue. Does the defense of extreme emotional disturbance require a completely subjective evaluation of reasonableness?

Held. No. Judgment affirmed.

- Under the criminal statute, modeled after the Model Penal Code, D has the burden of proof as to the affirmative defense of extreme emotional disturbance. The defense is broader than the traditional "heat of passion" defense that it replaced, because extreme emotional disturbance need not be spontaneous; it may affect the accused's mind for a substantial period of time before becoming manifest.

- There are two elements to the defense of extreme emotional disturbance: (i) an act done under the influence of extreme emotional disturbance; and (ii) a reasonable explanation for the disturbance as viewed by a person in the defendant's situation under the circumstances as the defendant believed them to be.

- D claims that the extreme emotional disturbance defense is based on a subjective standard of reasonableness. The first element of the defense is clearly subjective, but the second requires an objectively reasonable explanation. The jury evaluates the defense by viewing the accused's internal situation and his perception of the external circumstances, and then determining whether from that viewpoint the explanation for the emotional disturbance is reasonable. By this means, an accused has a fair opportunity for mitigation, while the fact finder is not required to find mitigation whenever emotional disturbance exists.

- The trial court applied the correct standard when it considered D's mental disability but found that D's excuse was so peculiar to him that it did not merit mitigation. D acted out of malevolence, not pursuant to an understandable human response that deserves mercy.

C. UNINTENTIONAL KILLINGS: UNJUSTIFIED RISK-TAKING

1. **Introduction.** Involuntary manslaughter is an unintentional homicide committed without excuse, justification, or malice. Involuntary manslaughter may result from the commission of a lawful act in a negligent manner, or from the commission of an unlawful act that is not a felony (the misdemeanor-manslaughter rule).

   a. **Criminal and tort negligence compared.** Most states require a higher degree of negligence for criminal liability than that required for ordinary (tort) negligence. The negligence required has either one or both of the following two elements:

      (i) The defendant's conduct must involve a high degree of risk of death or serious bodily injury in addition to the unreasonable risk required for ordinary negligence.

      (ii) Whatever the degree of risk required, the defendant must be aware that his conduct creates this risk.

      Note that if both are required, then "recklessness" is a more appropriate term than negligence.

2. **Unlawful Act Doctrine.** "Unlawful act involuntary manslaughter" covers an unintentional homicide in the commission of a dangerous, unlawful (malum

in se) act. If the unlawful act is "malum prohibitum," the defendant generally is held not guilty of manslaughter unless the death is the foreseeable consequence of his conduct in committing the act. Thus, if A ran into B, a pedestrian, while driving in excess of the speed limit (although not recklessly), she would not be guilty of involuntary manslaughter since the act is only "malum prohibitum," not "malum in se."

3. **Dangerous Pets--**

Berry v. Superior Court, 256 Cal. Rptr. 344 (Cal. Ct. App. 1989).

Facts. Berry (D) kept a pit bull dog in his yard. D bought the dog from a breeder of fighting dogs, and D had considerable literature and equipment for dog fighting. D kept the dog tethered behind a fence, but the fence did not completely surround the dog. The dog apparently protected marijuana plants that D grew in his backyard. D's house was on the same lot as the house of a family with four children. One of the children, James, then two years and eight months old, was playing in his yard while being watched by his mother. She went inside for about one minute, and when she came out, James was gone. James's father found D's dog mauling James, who died from the injuries. D was charged with murder and seeks dismissal of the murder charges.

Issue. May implied malice be found when a defendant keeps a dangerous dog that kills a person?

Held. Yes. Petition denied. [*Editor's Note*: The casebook does not include the holding because it presents the case as a problem for the student to decide the verdict.]

♦ Implied malice in an unintentional killing is actual appreciation of a high degree of risk that is objectively present. The act must be done with wanton disregard for life and a base antisocial motive, with a high probability that it will result in death.

♦ The evidence in this case shows that D was actually aware of his dog's potential danger to humans. He kept it chained and spoke about its dangerousness, as well as his knowledge of the breed, which is known as being dangerous to humans. This evidence supports a finding of the existence of an objective risk and D's subjective awareness of the risk. The antisocial aspect of D's conduct is shown by the illegality of keeping a fighting dog and by the apparent purpose of guarding the marijuana.

♦ The probability that a death could result from D keeping the dog is a matter for the jury.

♦ D notes that he was also charged with the separate offense of keeping a fighting dog. This does not preclude a murder charge for the same conduct, however, because the fighting dog statute does not include the element of malice. A special statute does not replace a general statute unless it includes all the elements of the latter.

---

4. Definition of "Malice."

a. In *People v. Nieto Benitez*, 840 P.2d 969 (Cal. 1992), the court discussed the meaning of the word "malice," noting that second degree murder requires a finding of malice aforethought, while manslaughter requires a finding that the killer acted without malice. The court recognized that, under California law, malice is express when there is manifested a deliberate intention unlawfully to take a life and implied when no considerable provocation appears or where the circumstances show an "abandoned and malignant heart." The mental state comprising malice is independent of that encompassed by the concepts of willfulness, deliberation, and premeditation needed for a finding of first degree murder. The court found the phrase "abandoned and malignant heart" to be too cryptic, preferring instead the explanation that "malice may be implied when defendant does an act with a high probability that it will result in death and does it with a base antisocial motive and with a wanton disregard for human life."

b. Under the Model Penal Code, ordinary recklessness is sufficient for a finding of manslaughter, while a finding of murder requires the additional judgment that the actor's conscious disregard of the risk manifested "extreme indifference to the value of human life." [Model Penal Code §210.2(1)(b) (1985)]

5. Awareness of Effects of Alcohol--

State v. Hernandez, 815 S.W.2d 67 (Mo. Ct. App. 1991).

Facts. Hernandez (D) drove his van around a curve, with two of the vehicle's wheels off the ground, and into the wrong lane of travel. Butcher, who was driving a truck on the same highway, applied his brakes and pulled his truck as far to the right as possible. D's van returned to the proper lane but then came back into Butcher's line of traffic and collided with Butcher's truck. One witness, an employee of an ambulance service, attended to D and asked whether he had been drinking. D replied that he had drunk "a 12-pack and some whiskey." Butcher and his son were injured in the accident, and his passenger, Barrymore, was pronounced dead at the scene. The sun visor and a sticker from the back window of D's van were admitted into evidence over D's objection. Stickers and pins on the visor and the sign from the window each contained slogans condoning heavy drinking, such as "Reality is for those who can't stay drunk," "The more I drink, the better you look," and "I only drink to make other people more interesting." A jury found D guilty of involuntary manslaughter. D appeals.

Issue. Is evidence of drinking slogans displayed on a defendant's vehicle relevant in an involuntary manslaughter case?

Held. No. Judgment reversed.

- In order for evidence to be relevant, it must logically tend to support or establish a fact or issue between the parties. Here, evidence of the drinking slogans is only admissible if it tends to support or establish either or both of the elements of involuntary manslaughter, *i.e.*, that the defendant acted with criminal negligence and, in doing so, caused the decedent's death.

- The state argues that the drinking slogans are relevant because they show that the defendant knew excessive drinking would impair him. This knowledge, however, is not at issue. The essence of manslaughter is the defendant's lack of awareness of the risk to others from his conduct. The slogans also were inadmissible to show bad character, as D had not put his reputation in issue.

Dissent. The definition of criminal negligence under the state statute is derived from section 2.02 of the Model Penal Code. Under this section of the Code, the jury must consider the circumstances known to the defendant in deciding whether to condemn his lack of awareness. Here, the jury should be able to consider circumstances known to D, including his knowledge of how consuming alcohol would affect his ability to drive. At least three of the slogans in question logically relate to D's knowledge of how alcohol could affect him, and were thus properly admitted. The admission of the remaining slogans was harmless.

---

6. Objective and Subjective Standards--

State v. Williams, 484 P.2d 1167 (Wash. Ct. App. 1971).

Facts. The Williamses (Ds), husband and wife, were both Indians who did not graduate from high school. The wife had two children from a prior marriage, the younger of whom was 14 months old. This child developed a toothache from an abscessed tooth. Within a two-week period, an infection of the mouth and cheeks developed and became gangrenous. Because he could not eat, the child's resistance was lowered and he contracted pneumonia, from which he died. During this time, Ds knew that the child was ill, and they gave him aspirin. They did not take him to a doctor for fear that the authorities would keep him because of his condition. The autopsy surgeon testified that, even if the child had seen a doctor in the last week, the child's life could not have been saved. Ds were charged with manslaughter for negligently failing to provide necessary medical attention. Ds were convicted and now appeal.

Issue. May ordinary negligence suffice to render a person criminally liable?

Held. Yes. Judgment affirmed.

- The common law rule required more than ordinary or simple negligence for a determination of involuntary manslaughter; gross negligence was essential. A Washington state statute has modified the law by imposing criminal liability where death is the proximate result of only simple or ordinary negligence.
- Ds were required to exercise ordinary caution. They knew that the child was sick while there was still time to take him to a doctor and save his life. They had taken him to a doctor previously. They could see that his condition was deteriorating. Ds breached their duty of caution, and the child died as a proximate result of the breach. Thus, they are guilty.

D. UNINTENTIONAL KILLINGS: UNLAWFUL CONDUCT

1. **The Felony-Murder Rule.** At common law, any homicide committed while perpetrating or attempting to perpetrate a felony was murder. Most jurisdictions have limited this rule.

   a. **Types of felonies.** Some jurisdictions have amended the felony-murder rule to hold that it will be applied only to certain types of felonies (*e.g.*, rape, robbery).

   b. **"In perpetration of" felony.** The homicide must occur "in the perpetration of" the felony. Most courts interpret this to mean that it is sufficient if the homicide takes place at any time within the "res gestae" of the other felony, and this includes all acts in the immediate preparation, actual commission, and immediate escape. A few courts require that the homicide occur at the actual moment of technical perfection of the felony (*e.g.*, if the felony is burglary, it must occur during the breaking and entering).

2. **The Doctrine in Its Unlimited Form--**

People v. Fuller, 150 Cal. Rptr. 515 (Cal. Ct. App. 1978).

Facts. While on routine patrol at 8:30 a.m. on a Sunday morning, police officer Ballesteroz approached a Dodge car lot, saw an older model Plymouth parked in front of the lot, and observed the defendants (Ds) rolling two tires apiece toward the Plymouth. He radioed for a unit to be dispatched to the scene. As Ballesteroz continued driving, Ds got into the Plymouth and drove away quickly, leading to a high-speed chase that ended with Ds running a red light and striking another vehicle, killing its driver. Later investigation revealed that four locked vans at the Dodge lot had been forcibly entered and the spare tires removed, and Ds' fingerprints were found on the jack stands in some of the vans. At Ds' trial, the court struck the murder count premised on the felony-murder rule. The state appeals.

Issue. Does the felony-murder rule apply to an unintentionally caused death during a high-speed automobile chase following the commission of a nonviolent, daylight burglary of an unattended motor vehicle?

Held. Yes.

- ♦ State law provides that a killing committed in the perpetration of burglary or certain other specified offenses constitutes first degree murder. Here, Ds committed burglary and Ds' actions in the course of the burglary led to the death of the deceased. Thus, Ds can be prosecuted for first degree murder.

- ♦ If we could rule differently, we would, however, because the burglary Ds committed was not dangerous to human life. Ds burglarized unoccupied vans parked on an empty lot, and they were not armed and presumably had no expectation to use violence. This result is too harsh.

Comment. The court might have avoided its undesired outcome if it had found that the killing was not committed in the perpetration of the burglary.

---

3. **The Policy Debate.** The felony-murder rule is widely criticized, and some states and countries have abolished it. Courts that do apply the rule often rationalize it under theories of deterrence, transferred or constructive intent, retribution, or general culpability.

4. **Limitations on the Rule.**

    a. **The "inherently dangerous felony" limitation--**

People v. Howard, 104 P.3d 107 (Cal. 2005).

Facts. Howard (D) was pulled over by police for driving without a rear license plate. When the police officers stepped out of their vehicle, D drove off. The officers chased D at speeds up to 90 miles per hour. During the chase, D turned off his car's headlines, ran several stop signs and red lights, and drove on the wrong side of the road. D eventually crashed into another vehicle and killed the driver. D was arrested and charged with murder and with violation of section 2800.2, evading a police officer in willful or wanton disregard for the safety of persons or property. D was convicted on both counts, and the court of appeal affirmed. D appeals, arguing that he could not be convicted under the second degree felony-murder rule because he did not commit an inherently dangerous felony.

Issue. Is the crime of driving with a willful or wanton disregard for the safety of persons or property while fleeing from a pursuing police officer an inherently dangerous felony for purposes of the second degree felony-murder rule?

Held. No. Conviction reversed.

- Murder is the unlawful killing of a human being, with malice aforethought. Under the second degree felony-murder rule, a defendant can be convicted without showing malice if the killing occurred during the commission of an inherently dangerous felony.

- This is a court-made rule, not found in statute. When determining whether a felony is inherently dangerous, the court looks to the elements of the felony in the abstract, not the particular facts of the case. Section 2800.2, defines "willful or wanton disregard for the safety of persons or property" to include ***any*** flight from the police during which the defendant commits three traffic violations that are assigned a "point count." These violations can include things like driving with a suspended license or making a right turn without signaling for 100 feet before turning. This type of conduct ordinarily would not be considered particularly dangerous. A violation of section 2800.2 is not, in the abstract, inherently dangerous to human life. Thus, the second degree felony-murder rule does not apply when a killing occurs during a violation of section 2800.2.

- This is not to say that a defendant who kills an innocent person during a high-speed chase cannot be convicted of murder. The jury may still find that the defendant acted with malice by driving with conscious disregard for the lives of others.

Concurrence. I agree that D's conviction must be reversed, but I would abrogate the second degree felony-murder rule entirely. Application of the rule is irredeemably arbitrary. Unlike the majority, I believe any high-speed pursuit is inherently dangerous. However, it should be left to the legislature to define precisely what conduct subjects a defendant to strict criminal liability.

Dissent. I am not persuaded by the majority's reasoning that, because some statutory "points" violations are not inherently dangerous, one can commit a violation of section 2800.2 in a way that does not place human life at risk. The principal reason for applying the felony-murder rule—deterrence—is present here.

---

b. The "independent felony" (or merger) limitation--

People v. Robertson, 95 P.3d 872 (Cal. 2004).

Facts. Robertson (D) fired shots at some men who were attempting to steal the hubcaps from D's vehicle. One of the men was shot in the foot, and another was shot fatally in the back of the head. D claimed that he did not intend to kill the men, but meant only to scare them away by shooting over their heads. At D's trial, the jury was instructed on first degree murder, second degree felony-murder based on the commission of the crime of discharging a firearm in a grossly negligent manner, and voluntary manslaughter. The jury convicted D of second degree murder. The court of appeals reversed, finding that the merger doctrine barred instruction on second degree murder based on a felony-murder theory. This appeal followed.

Issue. Does the merger doctrine bar instruction on second degree felony murder based upon the predicate offense of discharging a firearm in a grossly negligent manner?

Held. No. Conviction upheld.

- The felony-murder rule eliminates the need for proof of malice in connection with a charge of murder. The principal purpose of the rule is to deter felonies that put human life at risk.

- The merger doctrine states that the felony-murder instruction is not proper when the predicate felony is an "integral part of the homicide." The merger doctrine does not apply when the death results from a defendant's commission of a felony with an independent purpose. Here, D's admitted purpose in firing the gun was to frighten away the men who were vandalizing his automobile. Thus, the discharge of the firearm was undertaken with a purpose collateral to the resulting homicide.

Dissent. The majority mistakenly concludes that D had a felonious purpose independent of the killing. Under that rationale, D would have been better off had he testified to firing at the victim intending to hit him, because then the second degree felony-murder rule would not apply. An intent to scare a person by shooting at the person is not independent of the homicide because it is nothing more than the intent required for an assault, which is not considered an independent felonious purpose.

---

c. Killings "in the perpetration" or "in furtherance" of a felony--

---

State v. Sophophone, 19 P.3d 70 (Kan. 2001).

Facts. Sophophone (D) and others broke into a house, and the resident alerted the police. D began to run away but was caught and arrested. Another perpetrator, Sysoumphone, was chased by another officer. The officer ordered Sysoumphone to lie down and not move, but he fired at the officer, and the officer shot and killed him. D was charged with conspiracy, aggravated burglary, and felony murder. D moved to dismiss the felony-murder charges on the grounds that an officer had killed

Sysoumphone and that D had been in custody at the time of the killing, but D was convicted of all counts. D appeals.

Issue. Can a defendant be convicted under the felony-murder rule if the killing itself was actually committed by the lawful acts of a non-felon?

Held. No. Judgment reversed.

- The statute provides that first degree murder includes the killing of a human being "in the commission of, attempt to commit, or flight from an inherently dangerous felony [as defined elsewhere in the statutes]." [K.S.A. §21-3401] Aggravated burglary is an inherently dangerous felony. Time, distance, and the causal relationship between the felony and a killing may be considered in determining whether the defendant is subject to the felony-murder rule. Here, the killing took place during the flight from an aggravated burglary.

- Under the majority rule, the felony-murder rule does not apply if the person who directly causes the death is a non-felon, because only the acts of accomplices can be imputed to one another under the agency theory. An alternative approach, the "proximate causation" approach, holds that a felon may be held responsible if he set in motion the acts that resulted in the victim's death. We adopt the agency theory, which is in line with the strict construction we give the criminal statute.

Dissent. Nothing in the statute requires the court to adopt the agency theory. Here, D set in motion acts that could just as well have resulted in the death of a police officer as that of D's co-felon. I believe this is the type of case the legislature had in mind when adopting the felony-murder rule.

---

5. **Unlawful-Act Manslaughter (The "Misdemeanor-Manslaughter" Rule).** If an unintentional killing occurs during the course of a non-felony unlawful act, the killing falls into the category of common law involuntary manslaughter. This rule, too, has been subject to substantial criticism, and many courts have imposed limitations, *e.g.*, limiting it to killings resulting from malum in se conduct or the commission of dangerous misdemeanors.

E. CAPITAL MURDER

1. The Constitutional and Policy Debate.

a. **Introduction.** Under common law, crimes were classified as treason, felony, and misdemeanor. Crimes classified as felonies under common law were punishable by the death penalty. Although the penalties have changed, the offenses have generally retained that status under modern statutes. The type of penalty used today to distinguish a felony from a misdemeanor is usually the type of prison to which the offender may be sent or the length of sentence that can be imposed. Two other classifications continue in modern times: capital/noncapital crimes, and infamous/noninfamous crimes.

b. **Capital punishment constitutional--**

Gregg v. Georgia, 428 U.S. 153 (1976).

Facts. Gregg (D) was found guilty of murder and sentenced to death under Georgia law. In an earlier case, *Furman v. Georgia*, 408 U.S. 238 (1972), the Supreme Court had held the Georgia capital punishment statute unconstitutional because it allowed imposition of the death penalty in a capricious and arbitrary manner. D challenges the state statute as amended.

Issue. Is capital punishment per se "cruel and unusual punishment" and therefore unconstitutional under the Eighth and Fourteenth Amendments?

Held. No. Judgment affirmed.

- Although unappealing to many, capital punishment is essential to an ordered society that requires reliance on the legal process instead of self-help. On a number of occasions, we have both assumed and asserted the constitutionality of capital punishment. In fact, 35 states enacted capital punishment statutes since the *Furman* decision, indicating continued public acceptance of capital punishment.

- Because statistical attempts to evaluate the deterrent effect of the death penalty have been inconclusive, the resolution of this complex factual issue properly rests with state legislatures.

- Under Georgia's sentencing procedure, the jury's discretion is always circumscribed by legislative guidelines. The death penalty is available for only six categories of crime: murder, kidnapping for ransom or where the victim is harmed, armed robbery, rape, treason, and aircraft hijacking. After a verdict of guilty, a separate sentencing hearing is conducted, and the jury must find that one of 10 specified aggravating circumstances exists before imposing the death penalty. This satisfies the concerns of *Furman* as to those defendants who were being condemned to death capriciously and arbitrarily.

Concurrence (White, J., Burger, C.J., Rehnquist, J.). D indicts our system of justice by arguing that the amount of discretion involved in the imposition of the death penalty is unconstitutional. This is not an acceptable proposition of constitutional law. Although the imposition of the death penalty is a formidable responsibility, society must protect the lives of its citizens, and criminal laws against murder are necessary to achieve this goal.

Dissent (Brennan, J.). The fundamental premise of the Cruel and Unusual Punishment Clause is that all persons are human beings possessed of human dignity which must be preserved. The death penalty is unconstitutional as it treats certain humans as nonhumans, thereby degrading human dignity.

Dissent (Marshall, J.). The death penalty is unnecessary to promote the goal of deterrence or to further any legitimate notion of retribution, and is thus "cruel and unusual punishment."

---

2. **The Quest for Reliable Procedures.**

   a. **Introduction.** The Court in *Furman* indicated that a jury should not be granted unfettered discretion to make sentencing decisions in cases involving capital murder, while the Court in *Woodson v. North Carolina*, 428 U.S. 280 (1976) recognized a need to give juries some discretion, in view of the fact that defendants are "uniquely human beings." Many have noted that these two holdings cannot be reconciled.

   b. **The lingering question of racial discrimination--**

McCleskey v. Kemp, 481 U.S. 279 (1987).

Facts. McCleskey (D) was convicted of murder for killing a white police officer during the course of a robbery. D was black. D was sentenced to death based on the aggravating circumstances that the murder was committed during the course of an armed robbery and the victim was a police officer who was performing his duties. The state supreme court upheld the conviction and sentence. D then petitioned for a writ of habeas corpus in federal court, claiming that the capital sentencing process was racially discriminatory. To support his claim, D proffered a statistical study, the Baldus study, that showed that a black person convicted of killing a white victim was significantly more likely to be sentenced to death than a white person convicted of killing either a white person or a black person. The district court dismissed the petition, and the court of appeals affirmed. D appeals.

Issue. May an accused rely on statistical evidence of racial disparity in sentencing to prove that the sentencing procedure is unconstitutional?

Held. No. Judgment affirmed.

♦ A defendant claiming deprivation of equal protection must prove purposeful discrimination that had a discriminatory effect on him. D failed to prove that the decisionmakers acted with discriminatory purpose in this case. Instead, D relied on the statistical study. While statistics may be useful in some types of cases, they are inapplicable to capital sentencing decisions.

- Sentencing procedures require consideration of innumerable factors that depend on the facts of each particular case. An appropriate inference that would apply to a specific decision may not be drawn from general statistics. The sentencing procedure, as well as the entire criminal justice system, relies on discretion as a basic principle, and the exercise of such discretion should not be overturned by resort to general statistical analysis.

- Even if the procedure in individual cases results in statistical disparities, this does not show that the state had a discriminatory purpose in using the system. There is no evidence that the state legislature adopted the capital punishment statute to further a racially discriminatory purpose.

- D also claims that the sentencing system violates the Eighth Amendment. This attack on the discretionary nature ignores the substantial benefits to a defendant that accrue from the discretion in the system, such as the jury's ability to exercise leniency. The system is designed to minimize racial bias, while preserving the fundamental value of a jury and the benefits of discretion.

- Another problem with D's approach is that there is no limiting principle. D's claim of racial discrimination in the capital sentencing decision could be extended to other types of penalties or to claims by other minority groups. Also, D's claims are matters for the legislature, not the courts.

Dissent (Brennan, Marshall, Blackmun, Stevens, JJ.). D's chance of a death sentence was more likely because he was black. At some point before sentencing, D's lawyer probably had to tell D that he would likely receive the death sentence because of his race. Racial bias in the imposition of the death penalty is at odds with the need to evaluate a person as a unique human being. The greater willingness to impose the death sentence on black defendants, and the decreased willingness to impose the death sentence when the victims are black, reflects a devaluation of the lives of blacks. The Court's concern that accepting D's claim could lead to further claims involving other penalties and other minority groups does not take into consideration the different nature of the death penalty and the repugnance of racial discrimination. These should be considered when determining whether a punishment is cruel and unusual. The sophistication and strength of the Baldus study should also be taken into account.

---

c. **Victim impact evidence--**

Payne v. Tennessee, 501 U.S. 808 (1991).

Facts. Payne (D), having spent many hours doing cocaine and drinking beer, stabbed to death Charisse Christopher and her two-year-old daughter and nearly killed her three-year-old son, Nicholas, in Christopher's apartment after Christopher rejected D's sexual advances. The police stopped Payne, who was covered with blood, outside the apartment building and then discovered that the apartment unit was also covered with blood. D was convicted on two counts of first degree murder and one count of assault with intent to commit first degree murder. During the sentencing phase, D introduced the testimony of his parents and his girlfriend as to his good character and the testimony of a clinical psychologist as to his having a low I.Q. and a mental handicap. The state then presented the testimony of Christopher's mother that Nicholas was crying for his mother and sister and was hurt and confused. Arguing for the death penalty in closing argument, the prosecutor commented on the continuing effects of the crimes on Nicholas, pointing out that the boy was alive at the scene, had responded to paramedics, and was aware of what had happened. The jury sentenced D to death on both murder counts and to 30 years' imprisonment for the assault. D appeals.

Issue. Does the Eighth Amendment bar the admission of victim impact evidence during the penalty phase of a capital trial?

Held. No.

- ♦ Together, *Booth v. Maryland*, 482 U.S. 496 (1987), and *South Carolina v. Gathers*, 490 U.S. 805 (1989), held that such evidence, as well as a prosecutor's statements to the sentencing jury regarding the personal qualities of the victim, were per se inadmissible under the Eighth Amendment.
- ♦ We now believe, however, that a state may present such evidence to the jury as it elaborates on the specific harm the defendant caused. Just as the defendant has the right to be considered as an individual, the victim should also be considered as an individual whose death represents a unique loss to society and to her family.

Concurrence (Souter, Kennedy, J.J.). Every competent defendant knows that his crime will harm not just his victim but those close to his victim. The harm to such "survivors" is a foreseeable consequence of a successful homicidal act and is therefore morally relevant.

Dissent (Marshall, Blackmun, J.J.). Neither the law nor the facts supporting *Booth* and *Gathers* underwent any change in these last four years to warrant this abrupt change in opinion; only the personnel of the Court did.

Dissent (Stevens, Blackmun, J.J.). The evidence at issue here sheds no light on the defendant's guilt or moral culpability, thus serving no purpose other than to encourage jurors to follow their emotions rather than reason. The victim is not on trial. Thus, her character cannot constitute mitigating or, under other circumstances, aggravating, circumstances. We would not allow a defendant to show evidence that a victim was immoral. It is also incorrect to suggest that justice requires an even-handed balance between the state and the defendant. The Constitution grants certain rights to defendants and imposes certain limitations on the state to protect defendants.

3. Substantive Limitations on the Death Penalty--

Tison v. Arizona, 481 U.S. 137 (1987).

Facts. Three brothers, Donald, Ricky, and Raymond Tison, planned to help their father, Gary Tison, break out of prison. The brothers assembled a large cache of weapons, entered the prison, and left with their father and his cellmate, Greenawalt. After leaving the prison, they decided to abandon the car and steal another one. They flagged down a passing car occupied by John Lyons, his wife and two-year-old son, and his 15-year-old niece. Soon after, Greenawalt and Gary Tison shot and killed all four of them. Ricky and Raymond (Ds) were caught by the police and were later tried for capital murder of the four victims and for the associated crimes of armed robbery, kidnapping, and car theft. They were convicted of the four murders under Arizona's accomplice liability and felony-murder statutes and were sentenced to death. Arizona's felony-murder law provided that any killing occurring during the commission of a kidnapping or robbery was capital murder, and each participant in such crimes was responsible for the acts of his accomplices. Ds were sentenced to death and thereafter appealed. The Arizona Supreme Court affirmed, and the United States Supreme Court granted certiorari.

Issue. Does the Eighth Amendment prohibit the death penalty in the case of a defendant who was convicted of murder under a felony-murder statute if he did not actually kill the victim, but his participation was major and his mental state was one of reckless indifference to the value of human life?

Held. No. Judgments vacated and case remanded for a determination of Ds' state of mind.

- ♦ Ds claim that they had no intent to kill anyone and were surprised when the killings occurred. They argue that the imposition of the death penalty in this case is prohibited under *Enmund v. Florida*, 458 U.S. 782 (1982). In *Enmund*, we reversed the conviction of Enmund, the driver of a getaway car in an armed robbery of an elderly couple's home. In that case, Enmund was waiting in the car for his accomplice to come out when the accomplice killed the elderly couple. We found that Enmund's death sentence was disproportional to the crime of robbery-felony-murder under those circumstances. Furthermore, in surveying the felony-murder laws of the various states, we found that only eight states, including Florida, authorized the death penalty solely for participation in a robbery in which another robber kills someone.

- ♦ In *Enmund*, we held that neither the deterrent nor the retributive purposes of the death penalty would be advanced by imposing capital punishment on Enmund, because his participation in the murders was so attenuated and tangential. We based this finding on the fact that murders only rarely occur during the course of robberies and that, if such killings did occur, they only rarely resulted in the imposition of the death penalty absent a finding of intent to kill.

Because there was no showing that Enmund had any intent to kill, and because his involvement in the killing was so minimal, we found that the death penalty was excessive punishment.

- In this case, Ds' degree of participation was more than minor, and the record would support a finding of the culpable mental state of reckless indifference to human life. Ds brought an arsenal of weapons to the prison and handed these weapons to their father, whom they knew had killed a prison guard during the course of a previous escape attempt, and to Greenawalt, also a convicted murderer. They then flagged down a passing car, robbed its occupants, and then held them at gunpoint while Gary Tison and Greenawalt decided what to do with them. Ds stood by and watched while the four victims were killed and made no effort to assist them.

- In *Enmund*, we explicitly found the death penalty to be permissible in the case where a defendant had the intent to kill, and impermissible in the case where a defendant had no intent to kill and minimal participation in the events that led to the killing. The defendants in this case fall into neither category. The issue here is whether the Eighth Amendment prohibits imposition of capital punishment in the case where a defendant's participation is major and his mental state is one of reckless indifference to the value of human life.

- We will not attempt to delineate here the particular types of conduct and states of mind that will warrant the imposition of the death penalty. We hold that major participation in the felony committed, combined with reckless indifference to human life, is sufficient to satisfy the *Enmund* culpability requirement.

Dissent. (Brennan, Marshall, Blackmun, Stevens, JJ.). The felony-murder doctrine is a living fossil from a time when all felonies were punishable by death. Today, in most jurisdictions, a felon cannot be put to death for a murder that he did not commit, specifically intend to commit, or attempt to commit. However, in some jurisdictions, including Arizona, the death penalty can still be imposed under such circumstances, and the Court now justifies the imposition of the death penalty for recklessness. While some commentators and states have approved the death penalty for those who kill in circumstances manifesting an extreme indifference to the value of human life, that is not relevant to this case because here Ds did not kill. If a defendant has not killed, a finding that he nevertheless intended to kill seems indispensable to establishing capital culpability. A finding that the defendant acted with intent is qualitatively different from a determination that the defendant acted with reckless indifference to human life, because the reckless actor did not choose to bring about the killing as the intentional actor did. We must ensure that the punishment a person receives conforms to the choices that person has made.

Comment. In *Atkins v. Virginia*, 536 U.S. 304 (2002), the Court held that the execution of "mentally retarded" defendants violates the Eighth Amendment. While not expressly defining the term "mentally retarded," the Court held that such persons have a diminished capacity to process and understand information, to reason, to exercise self-control, and to understand the reactions of others to their actions. Thus, their handicap serves to diminish their culpability. In *Thompson v. Oklahoma*, 487 U.S. 815 (1988), the Court held that the execution of killers under the age of 16 is unconstitutional, and in *Stanford v. Kentucky*, 492 U.S. 361 (1989), the Court held that age may be a mitigating factor in deciding whether to sentence a 16- or 17-year-old killer to death.

VIII. RAPE

A. INTRODUCTION

Laws concerning rape have evolved along with the place of women in society. In a real sense, such developments reflect changes in our view of the victims rather than the crime. Unlike victims of other crimes, women were long held responsible for avoiding rape. Whether women were criticized for how they were dressed, or where they were walking, or the establishments they patronized, they were held accountable for their own victimization. For many years, various state penal codes defined rape as sexual intercourse under various circumstances "with a female not the wife of the perpetrator." This traditional exemption for husbands who forcibly raped their wives was only one of the failings found in many state penal codes. Others included the gender specific nature of the crime, as well as the degree of force or resistance required.

B. FORCIBLE RAPE

1. **Introduction.** The offense of rape generally consists of forcible nonconsensual sexual penetration. In the absence of force or threat of force, nonconsensual sexual penetration was traditionally a criminal offense only if the victim was underage, unconscious, or mentally incompetent. However, a minority of states now treat all nonconsensual intercourse as a criminal offense.

2. **Force and Nonconsent--**

State v. Alston, 312 S.E.2d 470 (N.C. 1984).

Facts. Alston (D) and the prosecuting witness, Brown, had been involved in a consensual sexual relationship for about six months. The relationship was characterized by occasional violence when D struck Brown for not doing what he wanted. Their consensual sexual relations also involved some violence. At times, Brown left the apartment she shared with D to stay with her mother before returning when D called her. Brown finally moved in with her mother on May 15 after D struck her for refusing to give him money. Subsequently, D called and visited Brown occasionally at the school she was attending, but they did not have sexual relations. On June 15, D showed up at Brown's school and blocked her path to the entrance. She refused to tell D where she had moved. D grabbed her arm and led her to the parking lot, where he released her when she promised to walk with him. She did not run away because she was afraid of D. The two walked for a long time talking about their relationship. At one point, D threatened to "fix" Brown's face to show her mother that he was not playing. D also told Brown that he had a right to make love to her again. They walked to the house of a friend of D's where D and Brown had made love in the past. They entered the house, and D and his friend went to the back of the house and talked, leaving Brown alone in the living room. D and his friend returned, and then D's friend left. D asked Brown if she was "ready." She replied that she would not go to bed with D. Nevertheless, the two had sex without Brown resisting, other than her statement that she did not want to. Brown made a complaint to the police that same day. On another occasion, the two had sexual relations again and spent the night together. Subsequently, D was charged with second degree rape for the June 15 incident. D appeals.

Issue. For a conviction of rape, must the prosecution offer substantial evidence of the defendant's actual or constructive force?

Held. Yes. Judgment reversed.

- Second degree rape requires vaginal intercourse with the victim both by force and against the victim's will. Consent is a complete defense so long as it is not induced by fear of violence.

- Where there is a prior continuing consensual sexual relationship, the state normally can show the victim's lack of consent to a specific act only with evidence of statements or actions by the victim that were clearly communicated to the defendant and that expressly and unequivocally indicated the victim's withdrawal of any prior consent and lack of consent to the particular act of intercourse. Brown's statement that she did not want to go to bed with D is substantial evidence of her lack of consent.

- However, the State did not offer substantial evidence of the element of force in this case. Although threats of serious bodily harm that reasonably induce fear, or circumstances giving rise to a reasonable inference that the victim was forced to have sexual intercourse are sufficient, here there was not substantial evidence of either actual or constructive force. The threats of force used by D on June 15 were not related to the act of sexual intercourse. Although Brown may have had a general fear of D because of his conduct on prior occasions, there is no evidence that D used force or threats to overcome Brown's will to resist.

Comment. This case has been criticized for ignoring the impact on the woman of her history of experiencing violence from her attacker. To some extent, the history of violence may have normalized the violence between the parties. Some argue that a history of violence is the functional equivalent of a threat, but not of nonconsent, so that the only requirement for rape where the parties have a history of violence is actual nonconsent as to the specific act alleged to be rape.

---

3. How Much Force? The Resistance Requirement--

Rusk v. State, 406 A.2d 624 (Md. Ct. Spec. App. 1979).

Facts. Rusk (D) met the prosecutrix (P) at a bar and asked her for a ride home. P agreed and drove D home. Upon arriving at D's house, D asked P to come up to his apartment. P refused, and D took her car keys. According to P, she then became afraid and agreed to go up to D's apartment. In the apartment, D left P to go to the bathroom, but P did not attempt to leave. When D came back, he sat on the bed and turned the light off. He then pulled P onto the bed and began to remove her blouse. At trial, P stated that she begged D to let her leave and began to cry. D kept saying "no" and began to lightly choke her. P testified that she then said, "If I do what you want, will you let me go without killing me?" D said that he would. P performed oral sex, and they then had sexual intercourse. D was convicted of rape and assault. D appeals the rape conviction, but he does not challenge the conviction of assault.

Issue. To support a rape conviction, must the victim show that she resisted the attack and that her resistance was overcome by force or that she was prevented from resisting by threats to her safety?

Held. Yes. Judgment reversed.

- In *Hazel v. State*, 157 A.2d 922 (Md. 1960), the court stated that force is an essential element of the crime of rape and, to support a conviction, the evidence must show that the victim resisted and her resistance was overcome by force or that she was unable to resist because of threats to her safety. In this case, the victim's testimony does not show that she resisted or that her fear overcame her attempt to resist or escape as required by *Hazel*.

- We do not agree with the argument that the issue of whether or not intercourse was accompanied by force or threats of force is one of credibility to be resolved by the trier of fact. In ruling on a motion to acquit, the trial judge must first determine that there is legally sufficient evidence for the jury to find that the victim was reasonably in fear. Here, the evidence is legally insufficient to conclude that D's words or actions created in the victim's mind a reasonable fear that, if she resisted, he would have harmed her or would have used force to overcome her resistance.

Dissent. The majority has substituted their own view of the evidence for that of the judge and jury, and in doing so, they have perpetuated myths about the crime of rape that have no place in our law today. The evidence was sufficient to show that D had intercourse with the victim against her will and without her consent. However, because of their notion that a victim must actively resist an attack upon her, the majority has confused force and lack of consent. This places the focus on the extent of the victim's resistance, rather than on the acts of her assailant. Although this is illogical and unique in the criminal law, it seems to be the current state of Maryland law. The judge and jury in this case, observing the witnesses and hearing their testimony, concluded that the extent of the victim's resistance and the reasons for her failure to resist further were reasonable. Yet a majority of this court, without the ability to see and hear the witnesses, has simply concluded that, in their judgment, the victim's fear was not reasonable.

Comment. In *State v. Rusk*, 424 A.2d 720 (Md. 1981), the court of appeals reversed *Rusk v. State*, holding that the reasonableness of the victim's apprehension of fear was a question of fact for the jury to decide. However, in his dissenting opinion, Judge Cole stated that, to support a conviction of rape, the evidence must show that the victim submitted to intercourse due to fear generated by something of substance. He asserted that a victim must use more than mere words to resist nonconsensual intercourse, unless her assailant has objectively manifested his intent to use physical force if she resists. Judge Cole maintained that Rusk did not act in a manner reasonably calculated to cause the victim to be so afraid that she did not resist.

---

4. Forcible Compulsion--

Commonwealth v. Berkowitz, 609 A.2d 1338 (Pa. Super. Ct. 1992).

Facts. Berkowitz (D) and the victim were students at the same college and had mutual friends and acquaintances. On the afternoon of the alleged rape, the victim went to D's dorm room, looking for his roommate. The roommate was not there, but D invited her to stay and hang out. D asked her to sit on the bed with him, but instead, she sat on the floor. After they talked for a while, D got off the bed and straddled and kissed her. She told D that she had to go to meet her boyfriend. D then lifted her shirt and bra and began fondling her. The victim said "no" and continued to say "no" while D undid his pants and tried unsuccessfully to put his penis in her mouth. The two stood up, and D locked the door. D then put the victim on the bed, removed her sweatpants and underwear from one of her legs, and entered her. She softly told D "no," but did not scream out. After D was finished, he said, "Wow, I guess we just got carried away." The victim retorted, "No, we didn't get carried away, you got carried away." She then left the room and ran downstairs to her boyfriend, who called the police. At trial, D testified that, at different times before the incident, the victim had talked to him in a sexually suggestive manner. He claimed that he thought that the victim wanted to pursue a sexual relationship with him and that when she said "no" during the incident, she moaned it passionately. The victim testified that she said "no" in a moaning kind of way because "it was just so scary," but she also stated that D did not threaten her. The jury convicted D of rape and indecent assault. D appeals.

Issue. Is evidence of an accuser's verbal resistance, without evidence of the accused's actual physical force or threat of force, sufficient to convict the accused of rape?

Held. No. Judgment reversed and case remanded for a new trial on the indecent assault charge.

- Under Pennsylvania statute, a person commits the crime of rape when he engages in sexual intercourse with a person who is not his spouse: (i) by forcible compulsion; (ii) by threat of forcible compulsion that would prevent resistance by a person of reasonable resolution; (iii) who is unconscious; or (iv) who is so mentally deranged or deficient that such person is incapable of consent. In *Commonwealth v. Rhodes*, 510 A.2d 1217 (1986), the Pennsylvania Supreme Court stated that forcible compulsion includes not only physical force or violence, but also moral, psychological, or intellectual force.

- Whether there is sufficient evidence to demonstrate beyond a reasonable doubt that an accused engaged in sexual intercourse by forcible compulsion or by the threat of forcible compulsion must be determined in each case based upon the totality of the circumstances. Some of the important factors to be considered in making that determination include the respective ages and the mental and physical conditions of the victim and the accused, the atmosphere and physical setting in which the incident took place, whether the accused was in a position of authority, domination, or custodial control over the victim, and whether the victim was under duress.

- In this case, there was no significant disparity between the ages of the victim and D. There was no evidence that the physical or mental condition of one of them differed significantly from the other. The atmosphere and physical setting were not coercive. D was not in a position of authority, domination, or custodial control over the victim. And there was no evidence indicating that the victim was under duress. Furthermore, D did not threaten the victim.

- Although both the victim and D testified that throughout the incident the victim repeatedly and continually said "no," there is no evidence that the victim could not have gotten up and walked out of the room without any risk of harm or danger. The legislature defined rape as sexual intercourse by forcible compulsion, not as nonconsensual intercourse. Evidence of the victim's verbal resistance is relevant to prove that the intercourse was against her will, but it is not sufficient evidence of forcible compulsion.

Comment. The Pennsylvania Supreme Court affirmed the judgment of the superior court, holding that the rape statute did not apply where the victim did not consent to sexual intercourse but there was no forcible compulsion. Largely in response to this decision, the Pennsylvania legislature enacted a sexual assault statute that criminalized nonforcible, nonconsensual intercourse.

---

5. Meaning of "Physical Force"--

State of New Jersey in the Interest of M.T.S., 609 A.2d 1266 (N.J. 1992).

Facts. C.G., a 15-year-old girl, lived with her family and M.T.S. (D), a 17-year-old boy. C.G. claimed to have awakened during the night with D on top of her, having already penetrated her. C.G. slapped D and told him to get off of her and leave, which D did. At trial, D claimed that the encounter had started consensually. Although the trial court did not find that C.G. had been sleeping, it found that she had not consented and that second degree sexual assault had been proven. The verdict was reversed by the appellate division. The state appeals.

Issue. Does nonconsensual penetration constitute sexual assault if it is not accompanied by some level of force more than that necessary to accomplish the penetration?

Held. Yes. Judgment reversed.

- Under the New Jersey Code of Criminal Justice, sexual assault is the commission of sexual penetration with another person with the use of physical force or coercion. The Code does not interpret the words "physical force," and there are a variety of possible meanings. When there are conflicting interpretations of a statute, courts seek the underlying intent of the legislature.

- Before the reform of rape law in New Jersey in 1979, the statutory definition of rape was the "carnal knowledge of a woman, forcibly and against her will." Force was determined by the victim's response. The victim's burden of proving that she resisted greatly minimized the importance of the forcible and assaultive character of the defendant's actions. Reformers pointed out that empirical research indicated that women who resisted forcible intercourse often suffered far more serious injury than those who did not. This research discredited the assumption that the most reasonable response to a rape was to resist to the best of a woman's ability. Reformers agreed that rape is a crime of violence, rather than a distinctly sexual crime, and that the focus should be on the forceful and assaultive nature of the defendant's conduct, rather than on the victim's response.

- Because of the similarity between sexual assault and other forms of assault and battery, to require that the crime of sexual assault include physical force as well as the force involved in an act of involuntary sexual penetration would be inconsistent with the legislative purpose of eliminating any consideration of whether the victim resisted. Under the reformed statute, any act of sexual penetration without the affirmative and freely given permission of the victim constitutes sexual assault, and physical force in excess of that inherent in the act of sexual penetration is not required. Thus, there is physical force if the defendant applies any amount of force against another in the absence of what a reasonable person would believe to be affirmative and freely given permission. That permission may be inferred from acts or statements reasonably viewed in light of the surrounding circumstances.

- In a case where there is no allegation of violence or force extrinsic to the act of penetration, the factfinder must decide whether the defendant reasonably believed that the alleged victim had freely given affirmative permission. Here, the trial court found that the victim had not consented to intercourse through her words or actions.

6. Withdrawn Consent--

People v. John Z., 60 P.3d 183 (Cal. 2003).

Facts. Laura, 17 years old, took a friend, Juan, to a party at the home of John (D). At about 8:00 p.m., Laura decided to leave, but D asked if he could talk with her. Laura went with D into his unlit bedroom, where they talked until Juan came into the room. D and Juan asked Laura if she had ever fantasized about having sex with two guys. She said that she had not, but sat on the bed while D and Juan undressed her. The boys then began touching her and engaging in foreplay activities with her. After a while, D left the room, and Laura had intercourse with Juan. When D came back into the room, Laura was sitting on the bed naked. D began kissing her, and she kissed him back. D then penetrated her. D, whose left hand was in a cast, did not threaten or hurt her; he asked her if she would be his girlfriend. Laura did not push him away or hit him, and she did not actually tell D that she did not want to have intercourse, but she did tell him that if he cared about her, "he should wait and respect that I don't want to do this." She told him three times that she had to go home. Instead of releasing her, D asked her to give him more time. The juvenile court found D guilty of forcible rape. D appeals.

Issue. Is the crime of forcible rape committed if the victim consents to the initial penetration by the defendant but then withdraws her consent during the act of intercourse and the defendant continues against the victim's will?

Held. Yes. Judgment affirmed.

♦ In *People v. Vela*, 218 Cal. Rptr. 161 (Cal. Ct. App. 1985), the court held that if the victim consents to intercourse at the time of penetration but later withdraws her consent, any use of force by her assailant past that point is not rape. The *Vela* court reasoned that because the essence of rape is the outrage to the female and the violation of her womanhood, if a female initially willingly consents to sexual intercourse, the penetration does not constitute a violation of her womanhood nor cause her outrage. However, there is no way to measure the level of outrage the victim suffers from being subjected to continued forcible intercourse after she withdraws her consent, and we must assume that her outrage is substantial. Furthermore, nothing in our rape law conditions the act of rape on the degree of the victim's outrage, and no California case has held that the victim's outrage is an element of the crime of rape. In *People v. Roundtree*, 91 Cal. Rptr. 2d 921 (Cal. Ct. App. 2000), the court held that rape is committed when a victim withdraws her consent during sexual intercourse but is forced to complete the act.

- In this case, the appellate court held that forcible rape is committed when sexual intercourse is accomplished against the victim's will by force or threat of bodily injury and that it is immaterial at what point the victim withdraws her consent as long as she communicates the withdrawal of her consent to the perpetrator and he ignores it. The evidence of Laura's initial consent to intercourse with D was not conclusive, but assuming that she impliedly consented, or at least refrained from objecting until D achieved penetration, substantial evidence shows that she withdrew her consent and communicated that withdrawal to D.

- D argues that when there is initial consent to intercourse, a man, having a primal urge to reproduce, should be permitted a "reasonable amount of time" in which to withdraw once the woman raises an objection to further intercourse. D's "primal urge" theory lacks supporting authority, and there is nothing in our statutes or case law suggesting that a defendant may continue the act of intercourse once his victim withdraws her consent. Moreover, in this case, D was given sufficient time to withdraw, but he refused to do so despite Laura's objections.

- We hold that the offense of forcible rape is committed when, during consensual intercourse, the victim objects and attempts to stop the act and the defendant forcibly continues despite her objection.

Dissent. I concur with the majority that clear withdrawal of consent nullifies any earlier consent and that an assailant's forcible continuation constitutes rape. However, in a postpenetration rape case, the prosecution must prove beyond a reasonable doubt that the victim clearly communicated the withdrawal of her consent and the defendant used force to continue the act of intercourse. In this case, the facts do not clearly establish that Laura was forced to continue. Furthermore, although D did not instantly respond to her statement that she needed to go home, the majority does not say how soon D should have desisted to avoid conviction. The majority also does not address whether persistence is the same as force, and the juvenile court does not appear to have considered whether persistence should carry the same penalty as forcible rape.

---

7. Mens Rea

a. **Introduction.** Rape is a difficult crime for the judicial system to address. Because it is one of the most violent and despicable crimes, fairness to victims and society in general requires effective enforcement. However, it is difficult to distinguish between truthful and false complainants. The necessary mens rea is not easily articulated, nor are the rules easily applied to specific cases.

b. **Mistake of fact--**

Commonwealth v. Sherry, 437 N.E.2d 224 (Mass. 1982).

Facts. A registered nurse worked at a hospital where Sherry, Hussain, and Lefkowitz (Ds) were doctors. The nurse attended a party hosted by Sherry and another doctor. While there, the nurse met Hussain and Lefkowitz. At trial, the nurse testified that at various times during the party, Ds made sexual advances toward her. Ds later grabbed her by her arms and took her outside, saying that they were going to Rockport. The nurse protested but did not physically resist because she believed they were kidding and would leave her alone. However, Ds took her to Lefkowitz's home in Rockport. The nurse asked to be taken home, but instead, Hussain carried her into Lefkowitz's house. They toured the house, and in a bedroom, Ds began to remove their clothes. The nurse protested, but each D in turn had intercourse with her. They then further sexually harassed her and made her bathe. Ds testified at trial that the nurse voluntarily accompanied them and consented to the acts of intercourse. Ds requested jury instructions that would have required the jury to find beyond a reasonable doubt that they had actual knowledge of the nurse's lack of consent. The trial judge did not give these requested instructions, and the jury convicted each D of rape. Ds appeal.

Issue. If mistake of fact as to the victim's consent is a defense to the crime of rape, must the mistake of fact be reasonable?

Held. Yes. Judgment affirmed.

- ♦ The trial judge correctly instructed the jury on the essential elements of proof required for a rape conviction, including the amount of force used by the defendant and the victim's reasonable fear.

- ♦ Ds' argument that mistake of fact is a defense to the crime of rape lacks the requirement that the accused acted in good faith and with reasonableness. In any event, whether a reasonable good faith mistake of fact as to the victim's consent is a defense to the crime of rape has never been decided in Massachusetts. We do not need to decide whether a reasonable and honest mistake to the fact of consent would be a defense, because the defendants did not request a jury instruction based on a reasonable good faith mistake of fact.

C. RAPE BY FRAUD OR NONPHYSICAL THREATS

1. Fraud in the Inducement--

Boro v. Superior Court, 210 Cal. Rptr. 122 (Cal. Ct. App. 1985).

Facts. Ms. R. received a phone call from a man calling himself "Dr. Stevens" (D). D informed her that a blood test had revealed that she had contracted a dangerous, perhaps fatal, disease and that the only way she could be treated was either by undergoing painful surgery costing $9,000 or by having intercourse with an anonymous donor who had been injected with a serum that would cure her. This "treatment" cost $4,500, but D said that he would accept a down payment of $1,000. Ms. R. elected the latter option and met D at a hotel, where she had intercourse with D. D was later charged with rape under a subdivision of the California rape statute that stated that rape occurs when "a person is at the time unconscious of the nature of the act, and this is known to the accused." D seeks a writ of prohibition to restrain further prosecution against him on the count of rape.

Issue. Can a defendant be convicted of rape when the victim understood and consented to the act of sexual intercourse even though she was deceived as to the reason for the act?

Held. No. Writ issued.

- The prosecution argues that the victim was "unconscious of the nature of the act" because of D's misrepresentation that it was a medical treatment, not simply sexual intercourse. It is true that if deception relates to the act itself (fraud in the factum), no consent can be given because the victim does not understand the nature of the act. For example, in *People v. Minkowski*, 23 Cal. Rptr. 92 (1962), a physician was convicted of rape for "treating" several patients for menstrual cramps by penetrating them first with a medical instrument, and then with his penis. However, the instant case is distinguishable from *Minkowski* because the victims in that case were not aware at the time that the defendant was having sex with them and did not consent to intercourse as part of their treatment. The present case is also distinguishable from those cases in which a perpetrator fraudulently has intercourse with a woman by impersonating her spouse. Under California statute, this constitutes rape because it involves fraud in the factum since the woman's consent is to an act of marital intercourse, while what is actually committed is an act of adultery.

- In contrast, with fraud in the inducement, the deception relates not to the thing done, but merely to some collateral matter. California courts do not recognize fraud in the inducement as negating consent. The instant case involves fraud in the inducement. D used fraud to induce the victim to consent to intercourse. The victim understood the nature of the act in which she was engaging and to which she gave her consent. The fact that consent was obtained through D's fraudulent misrepresentation comprises a crime of a different nature than rape committed against a person who is at the time unconscious of the nature of the act.

Comment. After *Boro*, the California legislature amended its laws, making inducement of consent by fraudulent representation with the intent to create fear a crime punishable by imprisonment.

2. **Nonphysical Threats.** In *State v. Thompson*, 792 P.2d 1103 (Mont. 1990), a high school principal was charged with forcing a student to engage in sexual intercourse by threatening to prevent her from graduating. The charges were dismissed, and the dismissals were affirmed on appeal. The reasoning was that the victim was not "forced" to submit to sexual intercourse because there was no physical compulsion and no use or threat of imminent bodily harm. While agreeing that the victim had been intimidated, the court declined to include intimidation within the definition of force. However, a number of states have criminalized coercing another person to submit to sexual intercourse, and the Model Penal Code includes a provision that criminalizes "gross sexual imposition." This felony occurs when a male compels a female to submit to sexual intercourse "by any threat that would prevent resistance by a woman of ordinary resolution."

D. RAPE SHIELD LAWS

1. **Introduction.** Because of the special difficulties involved in proving or disproving rape, the rules of evidence have been carefully considered in this area. Instructions about the complainant's credibility are carefully worded. Some corroboration of the complaint may be required. Special limitations on cross-examination also apply.

2. **Cross-Examination of the Victim.** Generally, character evidence is not admissible to prove conduct. Federal Rule of Evidence 608 allows such evidence for impeachment of a witness, but only under narrow restrictions. Formerly, a rape victim's character trait for unchastity could be used. Today, every state has adopted "rape shield" laws that generally bar evidence of the victim's unchastity on the issue of consent. Most jurisdictions also do not allow proof of unchastity by specific instances of consensual intercourse with persons other than the defendant.

3. **Rape Shield Laws and Defendants' Sixth Amendment Rights.** In *State v. Herndon*, 426 N.W.2d 347 (Wis. Ct. App. 1988), the court addressed rape shield laws and their effect on a defendant's Sixth Amendment rights to confront adverse witnesses and to present evidence. Rape shield laws deny a defendant in a sexual assault case the opportunity to examine the complainant concerning, or offer extrinsic evidence of, the complainant's prior sexual conduct with third parties or her reputation for sexual conduct. The reasons for rape shield laws are: (i) to prevent a defendant from harassing and humiliating the complainant; (ii) to exclude evidence that has no bearing on whether the complainant consented at the time in question; (iii) to keep the jury focused on the relevant issues; and (iv) to promote effective law enforcement, because a victim will more readily report and testify in sexual assault cases if she does not fear that her prior sexual conduct will be made public. Rape shield laws protect the complainant when the probative value of the evidence is outweighed by the potential prejudice to the complainant.

These laws have generally been held constitutional, and courts have usually held that a defendant's Sixth Amendment rights are not absolute. However, the rape shield laws must yield to a defendant's Sixth Amendment rights if the evidence shows a complainant's pattern of conduct similar to that in the case at hand or if it shows that the complainant may be biased or have a motive to fabricate the charges.

4. **Prior Public Acts of the Victim--**

People v. Wilhelm, 476 N.W.2d 753 (Mich. Ct. App. 1991).

Facts. Wilhelm (D) was accused of sexual assault. He claimed that the alleged victim consented. At trial, D sought to introduce evidence that, prior to the alleged assault, he and another witness had observed the victim expose her breasts to two other men in a bar and that she had allowed one of the men to fondle her breasts. The prosecution successfully argued that this evidence should be excluded under the rape-shield statute. D was convicted of third-degree criminal sexual conduct. D appeals.

Issue. Did the trial court abuse its discretion in prohibiting D from introducing testimony concerning the alleged public acts of the victim?

Held. No. Conviction affirmed.

- D claims that the public nature of the victim's activities should remove them from the protection of the rape-shield statute. We disagree. The statute does not make this distinction. One of the purposes of the law is to encourage victims to report crimes without fear of an inquisition into their sexual pasts.

- D also claims that the preclusion of the evidence deprived him of his right to confrontation. Again, we disagree. Evidence of the victim's sexual conduct with a third party is irrelevant to the issue of whether she consented to sexual intercourse with the defendant.

E. STATUTORY RAPE

The American legal system followed English law by adopting statutory rape as a strict liability offense. Before 1964, courts throughout the United States held that a defendant's mistake as to the victim's age was not a defense to statutory rape. Although there have been revisions of statutory rape laws throughout the country, in many jurisdictions, a defendant may still be convicted even if the victim appeared older than the age of consent, misrepresented her age, or initiated sexual contact. [*See* Garnett v. State, *supra*] Originally, statutory rape laws were gender-specific, only criminalizing sexual acts with young females. Despite the paternalistic view that females needed special protection, feminists supported statutory rape laws. Victorian feminists were concerned with the spread of venereal disease, the sexual abuse of young females, and child prostitution. However, influenced by the sexual liberation movement and the women's liberation movement of the late 1960s and early 1970s, feminists began to argue that gender-specific statutory rape laws perpetuated negative gender stereotypes and reinforced the double standard. These feminists urged that the laws be made gender neutral. Feminists' advocacy, along with other factors, brought about reform of statutory rape laws. Now a majority of jurisdictions have made statutory rape gender neutral. Nonetheless, gender-specific statutory rape laws have withstood constitutional attack on equal protection grounds because they protect girls from the harmful consequences of teenage pregnancy.

IX. GENERAL DEFENSES TO CRIMES

A. CATEGORIES OF DEFENSES

The word "defense" generally refers to a set of circumstances or conditions that might prevent a defendant from being convicted for an offense. "Failure of proof" defenses, such as mistake, involve a circumstance that negates an element required to establish the offense. "Offense modifications," which apply even if all elements of the offense have been established, show that the defendant did not cause the evil or harm that the statute was enacted to prevent. "Justifications" involve situations in which the harm sought to be prevented by the statute is outweighed by the need to prevent a greater harm. "Excuses" arise when certain conditions, such as the defendant's mental health, suggest that the defendant is not responsible for his own actions. "Nonexculpatory public policy" defenses, such as a statute of limitations or legal immunity, relieve a defendant from liability to further a societal goal.

B. BURDEN OF PROOF

1. Allocating the Burden of Proof--

Patterson v. New York, 432 U.S. 197 (1977).

Facts. Patterson (D) was charged with second degree murder and at trial raised the affirmative defense of extreme emotional disturbance, which, if successful, would result in a verdict of manslaughter. Consistent with New York law, the trial court instructed the jury that D had the burden of proving his affirmative defense by a preponderance of the evidence. The jury found D guilty of murder, and the appellate division affirmed. D appeals on the basis that requiring him to prove his affirmative defense is an improper shifting of the burden of persuasion from the prosecutor to the defendant and is therefore a violation of due process.

Issue. Is it unconstitutional under the Fourteenth Amendment's Due Process Clause for a state to require a criminal defendant to prove an affirmative defense that does not serve to negate any facts of the crime that the state is to prove in order to convict?

Held. No. Judgment affirmed.

- To recognize a mitigating circumstance does not thereby require the state to prove its nonexistence in each case in which the fact is put in issue, if in the state's judgment this would be too cumbersome, too expensive, and too inaccurate.

- However, the state may not shift the burden of persuasion with respect to a fact that the state deems so important that it must be either proved or presumed in order to convict a defendant of the crime.

Dissent (Powell, Brennan, Marshall, JJ.).

- The state may not shift the burden of proof to the defendant if the following two factors exist: (i) the factor at issue makes a substantial difference in punishment and stigma; and (ii) the factor in question historically has been held to be of great importance in the Anglo-American legal tradition.

- To avoid this two-step test by leaving a factor out of the statutory elements of a crime is to undermine the presumption of innocence and to establish form over substance.

---

2. **Burdens of Production and Persuasion.** Criminal trials involve two burdens of proof: the burden of production and the burden of persuasion. The burden of production belongs to the party who has the initial responsibility to introduce evidence supporting the matter at issue. For example, the prosecutor bears this burden as to the elements of the charged crime, and the defendant bears this burden as to any affirmative defenses. The burden of persuasion refers to a party's obligation to produce the degree of evidence required to prove the facts upon which she relies.

C. PRINCIPLES OF JUSTIFICATION

1. **Introduction.** Generally, an action may be justified if it (i) was necessary to further or to protect an interest at stake, and (ii) caused only such harm as was proportional or reasonable in view of the harm threatened or the interest sought to be furthered.

2. **Self-Defense.**

   a. **General principles.** Generally, a person is privileged to use such force as reasonably appears necessary to defend herself against an apparent threat of unlawful and immediate violence from another.

      1) **Duty to retreat.** Contrary to the common law position, most American jurisdictions no longer require the defendant to retreat before using deadly force. However, a substantial minority of states still adhere to the common law rule, requiring retreat before resort to the use of deadly force in self-defense. Of course, there is no duty to retreat where retreat cannot be done safely, or where the attack takes place in the defendant's own home.

2) **Aggressor's right to defense.** Generally, a person cannot use force to defend herself if she was the initial aggressor in the situation. By beginning the altercation, she forfeits her right to assert self-defense later. However, there are some situations in which a person, although an initial aggressor, may regain her right to act in self-defense.

a) **Nondeadly aggressor met with deadly force.** If the victim responds to the aggressor's use of nondeadly force with deadly force, the aggressor can use whatever force appears reasonably necessary (including deadly force) to repel the attack. The rationale is that because nondeadly force cannot be met with deadly force, the victim, by responding with deadly force, has threatened unlawful harm.

b) **Aggressor withdraws.** An aggressor may regain her right to act in self-defense by withdrawing from the affray. Ordinarily, the defendant must actually notify her adversary of the desire to desist, but some jurisdictions hold that even unsuccessful efforts to do so, if reasonable, will suffice.

(1) **Aggressor's duty to withdraw--**

United States v. Peterson, 483 F.2d 1222 (D.C. Cir. 1973).

Facts. Keitt and two others drove to the rear of Peterson's (D's) house and began removing the windshield wipers from D's wrecked car. D came out and protested, and a verbal fight ensued. D went back into his house, got a gun, and came back out. In the meantime, Keitt had returned to his car and was preparing to leave with his companions. D warned Keitt not to move. He also threatened to kill Keitt if he came into D's yard. Keitt left the car, challenged D, and then got a lug wrench, which he raised. Keitt advanced toward D, who warned that he would kill Keitt if he took "another step." Keitt did not stop, and D shot him in the face, immediately killing him. D was convicted of manslaughter. D appeals.

Issue. May an aggressor claim self-defense if he does not first withdraw from the conflict?

Held. No. Judgment affirmed.

- The general rule is that a claim of self-defense may not arise from a self-generated necessity to kill. Such a killing is not defensive because the necessity could have been averted. A claim of self-defense may arise, however, if the aggressor communicates to his adversary an intent to withdraw and then in good faith attempts to do so.

- Here, Keitt may have been the original aggressor, but he was about to leave or withdraw, when D challenged him with a gun. D never made an attempt to withdraw and, having become the aggressor, may not claim self-defense.

Comment. In *State v. Abbott*, 174 A.2d 881 (N.J. 1961), the court held that a person who is being attacked is required to retreat only if he intends to use deadly force.

---

b. **"Reasonable belief" requirement.** The defendant must have believed that the force used was necessary for her own protection, and this belief must have been reasonable (*i.e.*, a belief that a reasonable person in the same or similar circumstances would have formed). But, at the same time, an honest and reasonable belief is enough—the defense is still available even though it turns out that the belief was wrong and there was, in fact, no actual need to use force in self-defense.

1) **Threatened harm imminent.** The defendant must have reasonably believed that the threatened harm was imminent; *i.e.*, that it would be inflicted immediately if she did not act in self-defense. Thus, it is necessary to consider whether the threatening person was actually present and, if so, whether the person appeared willing and able to injure the defendant.

2) **Threatened harm unlawful.** The threatened harm must have been unlawful. This raises the issues of whether force can be used to resist an unlawful arrest and whether one who is the initial aggressor can claim the defense at all.

3) **Reasonable force.** The force that the defendant used must have been reasonable. In other words, it must have been no greater than appeared necessary under the circumstances to prevent the victim from inflicting the harm.

a) **Special limits on the use of deadly force.** "Deadly force" is force used with the intent to cause death or serious bodily injury or that is known by its user to create a substantial risk of death or serious bodily injury. Although there is no absolute prohibition against the use of deadly force in self-defense, there are some special limits on when it may be used.

b) **Perceived threat of death or serious bodily injury.** All courts agree that deadly force may be used in self-defense only if the defendant reasonably believed that the other person was about to inflict death or great bodily injury upon her and that deadly force was necessary to prevent the harm.

4) General requirements--

People v. Goetz, 497 N.E.2d 41 (N.Y. 1986).

Facts. Goetz (D) entered a subway car and sat on a bench. He was approached by two black youths, one of whom stated to D, "Give me five dollars." These two youths were accompanied by two others who were also in the subway car. D pulled out a handgun and fired four shots, hitting three of the youths. He then fired another shot at the youth he had missed, severing his spinal cord. D then told the conductor who responded that the youths had tried to rob him. D fled the scene, but turned himself in about a week later. D told the police that he was carrying a gun because he had been mugged and injured three years earlier and had successfully protected himself on two prior occasions by displaying the gun to would-be assailants. D also described his deliberate intent to hurt the youths and to shoot each of them, and stated that he would have shot more times if he had had more bullets. D was charged with attempted murder, assault, and weapons possession. The prosecutor instructed the grand jury that the defense of self-defense applies only when the defendant's beliefs and reactions are those of a reasonable person, an objective standard. D was indicted, but the appellate court reversed. The state appeals.

Issue. Must a claim of self-defense be evaluated based on what a reasonable person in the defendant's position would have believed?

Held. Yes. Judgment reversed.

- ♦ The use of force may be justified in certain circumstances, such as the defense of a person, but only to the extent the person "reasonably believes" the use of force to be necessary to defend himself from what "he reasonably believes" to be the use or imminent use of unlawful force by the aggressor. The use of deadly physical force is permitted only when the person "reasonably believes" that the aggressor is using or about to use deadly physical force or is committing or attempting to commit a robbery or other such violent crime.

- ♦ In explaining the meaning of the term "reasonably believes," the prosecutor stated that the jurors should consider whether D's conduct was "that of a reasonable man in D's situation." The lower court in reversing held that the statute requires consideration of whether D's reactions and beliefs were "reasonable to him," which is a subjective standard. This is incorrect.

- ♦ The common law required an objective standard of reasonableness when applying self-defense, and the legislature followed this approach when it modified the Model Penal Code section on self-defense. Whereas the Model Penal Code permits self-defense when the defendant believes that the use of deadly force is necessary, the New York statute requires that the defendant "reasonably" believe deadly force is necessary.

- An interpretation that permits a subjective standard would fundamentally change the law; it would allow a defendant to escape responsibility simply for believing that the actions taken were reasonable and necessary to prevent a perceived harm. Citizens are not free to set their own individual standards for the justifiable use of force.

- Even under the objective standard, however, the individual defendant's personal knowledge and experience must be considered when assessing the reasonableness of the defendant's belief.

---

5) Objective, subjective, or mixed standard?--

State v. Wanrow, 559 P.2d 548 (Wash. 1977).

Facts. Wanrow's (D's) two children were visiting the home of D's friend, Hooper. D's son, who had been playing outside, came back to Hooper's house and reported that a man had tried to pull him off his bicycle and drag him into a house. A few minutes later, Wesler appeared at Hooper's door, declaring, "I didn't touch the kid." Hooper's seven-year-old daughter saw Wesler at the door and indicated to her mother that Wesler was the man who had molested her some months earlier. As Wesler was leaving, Hooper's landlord told Hooper that Wesler had tried to molest a young boy who had earlier lived in the same house and that Wesler had previously been committed to a hospital for the mentally ill. Hooper suspected that it was also Wesler who had been prowling around her house recently and had slashed her bedroom window screen. Hooper called the police, but was informed that no arrest would be made before Monday morning. Hooper informed D of the developments, and D arrived with a pistol in her handbag. D and D's sister and brother-in-law stayed up all night at Hooper's house to protect the children. The brother-in-law, without the women's knowledge, went to Wesler's house with a baseball bat at 5 a.m. and accused Wesler of molesting children. Wesler suggested going to Hooper's house to straighten things out. Wesler entered the residence while the brother-in-law and a friend waited outside. Wesler, a large man who was visibly intoxicated, would not leave the home when requested. Shouting and confusion arose, waking a small child, and Wesler remarked, "My what a cute little boy." D, a woman on crutches, went to the door to enlist her brother-in-law's help, and upon turning around to reenter the living room, saw Wesler standing behind her. She testified to being gravely startled by the situation and having shot Wesler in a reflex action. D was convicted of second degree murder. D appeals.

Issues.

(i) Did the court err in instructing the jury to consider only those acts and circumstances occurring at or immediately before the killing in evaluating the gravity of the danger to D?

(ii) Did the court err in instructing the jury to consider whether D's conduct was objectively reasonable, using language suggesting that her conduct should be measured against that of a reasonable male?

Held. (i) Yes. (ii) Yes. Judgment reversed.

- The justification of self-defense is to be evaluated in light of all of the facts and circumstances known to the defendant, including those known substantially before the killing.

- D's actions are to be judged against her own subjective impressions, including such perceptions that are the product of our nation's history of sex discrimination.

---

6) **Battered women.**

a) **Self-defense--**

State v. Norman, 366 S.E.2d 586 (N.C. Ct. App. 1988).

Facts. Mrs. Norman (D) had been badly abused by her husband during most of their 25-year marriage. He frequently punched and kicked her, threw things at her, and burned her with cigarettes and hot coffee. He forced her into prostitution, humiliated her in public, and forced her to eat pet food from a bowl on the floor. For years he threatened to maim and kill her. This behavior continued until D shot her husband three times in the back of the head while he slept. The day before the killing, D was beaten to the point that police were summoned. However, the police would do nothing unless D took a warrant out on her husband, which she was afraid to do. At trial, two experts testified that D fit the profile of an abused or battered spouse who believed that killing the victim was necessary to avoid being killed. The court did not permit an instruction on self-defense. D was convicted of voluntary manslaughter. D appeals.

Issue. Under the facts of this case, does the victim's passiveness at the moment of the homicidal act preclude the defendant from asserting self-defense?

Held. No. New trial granted.

- The evidence was sufficient to submit an issue of self-defense to the jury. The evidence of the victim's repeated abuse plus the opinions of the experts would permit a jury finding that D believed it necessary to kill the victim to avoid her own death or serious bodily injury. The record would also permit a finding that D's belief was reasonable under the circumstances in which she found herself. Given the characteristics of battered spouse syndrome, a battered person need not in all cases wait until a deadly attack occurs to act in self-defense. Finally, the expert testimony considered with the other evidence would permit a reasonable inference that D used no more force than reasonably appeared necessary to her under the circumstances to protect herself from death or great bodily harm.

---

b) Requirement that threat of harm be "imminent"--

State v. Norman, 378 S.E.2d 8 (N.C. 1989).

Facts. (*See* State v. Norman, *supra.*) Judgment of the court of appeals was stayed for discretionary review by the Supreme Court of North Carolina.

Issue. Would the evidence in this case support a finding that D killed her husband due to a reasonable fear of imminent death or great bodily harm as required for an instruction on self-defense?

Held. No. Judgment reversed.

- The "imminence" requirement ensures that deadly force will be used only where it is necessary as a last resort in the exercise of the inherent right of self-preservation.
- The evidence here shows no danger of imminent death or bodily harm. The deceased was sleeping at the time D shot him three times in the back of his head. D was not faced with an instantaneous choice between killing her husband or being killed or seriously injured. Instead, she had ample time and opportunity to resort to other means of preventing further abuse.

Dissent. The evidence presented showed a 20-year history of beatings and dehumanizing treatment suffered by D, who believed escape was impossible. She reasonably believed that the law could neither help nor protect her. D could reasonably believe that the next potentially fatal attack was imminent, especially in view of how the husband's behavior had worsened during the three days prior to the shooting.

Comment. Two months after D entered prison to serve a six-year sentence, her sentence was commuted by the governor.

---

3. Defense of Others--

People v. Kurr, 654 N.W.2d 651 (Mich. Ct. App. 2002).

Facts. Kurr (D) and her boyfriend, Pena, had been arguing over Pena's cocaine use. Pena then punched D two times in the stomach, and she warned him not to hit her because she was carrying his babies. When Pena came toward her again, she stabbed him in the chest. Pena died as a result of the stab wound. Prior to trial, D successfully moved for permission to present testimony that she killed Pena in defense of her unborn children. At the conclusion of the trial, however, the court disallowed a defense of others instruction, noting that the fetuses would have been only 16 or 17 weeks in gestation at the time of the stabbing and that expert testimony had revealed that a fetus under 22 weeks old is nonviable. The court concluded that a defense of others theory requires the existence of a viable human being. D was convicted of voluntary manslaughter. D appeals.

Issue. Should D have been allowed a defense of others instruction?

Held. Yes. Judgment reversed and case remanded for new trial.

- In this state, the defense should extend to the protection of a fetus, viable or nonviable, from an assault against the mother. Our state has previously adopted a fetal protection act that punishes those who kill or harm fetuses or embryos at any stage of development under various circumstances, including during intentional assaults against pregnant women. Thus, the legislature has concluded that fetuses are worthy of protection as a matter of public policy. This policy should be extended to the defense of others concept when a pregnant woman is assaulted.

- In this case, the failure to give a defense of others instruction deprived D of her due process right to present a defense. It was insufficient to include a self-defense instruction and permit evidence of the pregnancy, as a jury could conclude that punches to D's stomach were insufficient to give her a right to defend herself, while at the same time concluding that they were adequate to give her a right to defend her unborn children.

---

4. **Defense of Property and Law Enforcement Defenses.**

   a. **Protection of property.** The right to use force in the protection of property is much more limited than the right to use force in the protection of persons.

      1) **Deadly force not allowed.** A person cannot use deadly force simply to defend her property against unlawful interference, even if there is no other way to prevent the threatened harm. This rule is based on the premise that the interest in security of property does not justify jeopardizing the lives of others.

      2) **Nondeadly force.** Nondeadly force may be used to protect both real and personal property in one's possession if it reasonably appears necessary to prevent or terminate an unlawful intrusion on or interference with that property.

a) **Request to desist.** But force is not reasonable unless a prior request has been made for the other to desist from interfering with the property.

3) **Property in possession of another.** Moreover, the traditional rules apparently require that the property defended be in the possession of the person using the force. Thus, there is probably no right to use force in defense of property in the possession of another.

4) **Compare—use of force to regain or reenter property.** Traditionally, one illegally dispossessed of property cannot use force to regain it or, in the case of real property, to reenter it. An exception is made, however, where action is taken immediately after the loss of the property or in "hot pursuit" of the dispossessor.

5) **Use of mechanical device--**

People v. Ceballos, 526 P.2d 241 (Cal. 1974).

Facts. Ceballos (D) lived alone both in a garage and in an apartment above the garage. D had some tools stolen from his home and a few months later noticed pry marks on one of the garage doors. One of the locks had also been bent. D set up a trap gun. Two boys who decided to break in and see if there was anything to steal opened the door. The gun fired and hit one of the boys in the face. D was convicted of assault with a deadly weapon. D appeals, claiming that the trap gun was justified.

Issue. May a person use a trap gun to protect property in his home while he is away?

Held. No. Judgment affirmed.

- The general rule imposes criminal and civil liability for setting up a deadly mechanical device that actually kills or injures another. An exception has arisen when the intrusion is such that the person, if present, could inflict the harm with his own hands. That exception should not apply to criminal cases, however, because under it, liability depends on fortuitous events, and because the use of trap guns presents an unacceptable danger to children, firefighters, etc.

- Even if the exception applied, D would be liable. Although homicide is justifiable as a defense against a forcible and atrocious crime, the burglary by the boys here did not threaten death or serious injury to anyone as they were the only persons present. Nor can the use of deadly force be justified solely for the protection of property.

---

b. **Law enforcement.** The dangers of law enforcement present many difficult questions as to the scope of justified violence. Problems arise when citizens assist law enforcement officers, when officers effectuate arrests, and when suspects resist arrest.

1) **Assistance to police.** Citizens may properly assist law enforcement agencies in good faith. However, the use of force as part of such assistance could endanger others. The defense of aiding law enforcement agencies does not exonerate a citizen from all liability for his conduct. The defense essentially nullifies criminal intent. The factfinder must scrutinize the defendant's conduct to determine whether it shows a lack of criminal intent. A private citizen called upon by a police officer to assist in making an arrest, however, has the same privilege as the officer because the citizen is required by law to comply with the police officer's order.

2) **Effectuating arrest.** Both private citizens and police officers may use force in making an arrest, but different standards apply to the two groups.

   a) **Police officers.** A police officer is entitled to act on reasonable appearances in using force to make an arrest. A police officer may use whatever nondeadly force reasonably appears necessary to make an arrest for a felony or misdemeanor. The right to use deadly force has traditionally been limited to situations in which the officer reasonably believes that the suspect committed a felony. The modern approach is more restricted; deadly force is permitted only if the suspect has committed a dangerous felony or presents a significant risk of harm to others.

   b) **Modern approach: Use of deadly force to stop fleeing burglar not permitted--**

Tennessee v. Garner, 471 U.S. 1 (1985).

Facts. The Tennessee fleeing felon statute authorized police officers to use deadly force to capture unarmed suspects fleeing from nonviolent felonies. One night, an unarmed 15-year-old boy broke into an unoccupied house to steal money and property. Two police officers responded and one, Officer Hymon, yelled at the boy to stop as he fled. As the boy tried to get over a fence, the police shot and killed him. Garner (P), the boy's father, sued Hymon, the police department, the mayor, and the city of Memphis for wrongful death. The state of Tennessee (D) intervened to defend the statute. The district court upheld the state law, but the court of appeals reversed. D appeals.

Issue. May a state authorize police officers to use deadly force to capture an unarmed suspect fleeing from a nonviolent felony?

Held. No. Judgment affirmed.

- Under Tennessee law, once it is determined that an officer could not have caught a felon without shooting, shooting is reasonable. The nature of the felony or the actual dangerousness of the felon is irrelevant.

- The Fourth Amendment protects against unreasonable seizures. Killing a fleeing suspect is certainly a "seizure" of the person. Under common law, killing a felon who resisted arrest was permitted, but at that time, all felonies were capital crimes, punishable by death. Thus, the use of deadly force against a fleeing felon resulted in the same outcome as the authorized punishment.

- Today, however, almost all of the crimes that were formerly punishable by death no longer are. Furthermore, the distinction between misdemeanors and felonies are now often minor, and some misdemeanors (*e.g.*, drunken driving) pose more of a physical threat than some felonies (*e.g.*, white collar crime). An important trend away from the use of deadly force to apprehend a non-dangerous fleeing felon is that of police departments in a majority of the large cities of the United States. This suggests that such a policy does not hamper effective law enforcement.

- In this case, Hymon did not think that the boy was armed and had no probable cause to think that he posed any threat. Hymon acted to prevent him from escaping, but this did not justify the use of deadly force under the Fourth Amendment. The Tennessee statute is unconstitutional in such a case.

Dissent (O'Connor, J., Burger, C.J., Rehnquist, J.). The reasonableness of the officer's seizure of the boy depends on the public interest involved and the intrusion on the boy's legitimate interests. The public interest in using deadly force to apprehend a fleeing burglar relates to the seriousness of the crime. Burglary is a serious and dangerous felony, and the public has a compelling interest in preventing and detecting burglaries. Apprehension of the suspect is critical. On the other hand, while a suspect has an obvious interest in his life, he does not have a right to flee unimpeded from the scene of a burglary. Use of deadly force as a last resort to apprehend a fleeing burglar at night is not unreasonable.

---

5. Necessity ("Choice of Evils").

a. General principles--

Nelson v. State, 597 P.2d 977 (Alaska 1979).

Facts. Shortly after midnight, Nelson (D) drove his truck onto a side road off a highway and became stuck in a marshy area. D was afraid the truck might tip over, and he and his two companions, Stinson and Thompson, spent an hour unsuccessfully trying to free the vehicle. Around 1 a.m., D and Stinson began walking down the highway and met up with an acquaintance, who drove them to a Highway Department Yard, marked with "no trespassing" signs, where heavy equipment was parked. After waiting several hours for someone to come by, they decided to take a dump truck to help free D's vehicle. The dump truck also became stuck. At approximately 10 a.m., Curly, a man whose vehicle was stuck further down the highway, offered to help D, and they returned to the yard and took a front-end loader. They used the loader to free the dump truck and the dump truck to free Curly's truck. They returned the dump truck to the yard and attempted to use the loader to free D's truck, but the loader became stuck. Exhausted, D and his companions went to sleep, one in D's truck. They were awakened by a Highway Department employee, who placed them under citizen's arrest. The dump truck and the loader sustained considerable damage as a result of D's actions to free his truck. D was convicted of reckless destruction of personal property and of joyriding. D appeals.

Issue. Did D make a case for the defense of necessity?

Held. No. Judgment affirmed.

- The defense of necessity may be raised if the defendant's actions, though unlawful, were necessary to prevent an even greater harm from occurring. There are three essential elements to the defense: (i) the act charged must have been done to prevent a significant evil; (ii) there must have been no adequate alternative; and (iii) the harm caused must not have been disproportionate to the harm avoided. The instruction given to the jury in this case adequately described these requirements.

- D is correct that the necessity defense is available if a person acted in the reasonable belief that an emergency existed and there were no alternatives available, even if that belief was mistaken. The person's actions should be weighed against the harm reasonably foreseeable at the time, rather than the harm that actually occurs. To the extent that the instruction given in this case did not adequately convey these concepts to the jury, however, such error was harmless, because D failed to make out a case for the necessity defense. By the time D appropriated the equipment, the truck had been stuck for hours without tipping over, suggesting that there was no true "emergency." Moreover, the record shows that many passersby stopped to offer help in the form of physical assistance, rides, or calls to state troopers or a towing company, revealing that D had lawful, adequate alternatives. Finally, D's actions were disproportionate to the situation he faced.

---

b. Civil disobedience--

United States v. Schoon, 971 F.2d 193 (9th Cir. 1991).

Facts. Schoon (D) was one of 30 people who gained admittance to the Tucson IRS office where they chanted "Keep America's tax dollars out of El Salvador" and splashed simulated blood on counters, walls, and carpeting, obstructing office operations. They refused to disperse when so ordered by a federal police officer. At trial, D attempted to assert a necessity defense, contending that they had acted to avoid further bloodshed in El Salvador. The trial court precluded the necessity defense, and D was convicted of obstructing the activities of the IRS office and failing to comply with an order of a federal officer. D appeals.

Issue. May a defendant who is charged with indirect civil disobedience raise the defense of necessity?

Held. No. Judgment affirmed.

- A necessity defense must show that one: (i) was faced with a choice of evils, and chose the lesser; (ii) acted to prevent imminent harm; and (iii) reasonably anticipated a direct causal relationship between the conduct and the harm to be averted. The trial court held that there was no immediacy, that the action taken would not have abated the evil, and that other legal alternatives existed.

- Direct civil disobedience involves protesting a law by breaking that law. Indirect civil disobedience involves violating a law or interfering with a government policy that is not, itself, the object of the protest. In addition to agreeing with the trial court's reasoning, we find that D engaged in indirect civil disobedience, because the group was not challenging the laws under which they were charged.

- The necessity defense requires that the commission of a crime avert the occurrence of an even greater harm. For example, prisoners may escape a burning prison. But we assume in such cases that the lawmaker, if confronted with such facts, would have carved out the exception which is subsequently claimed as justified by necessity.

- Indirect civil disobedience, however, involves the breaking of a law (other than the one sought to be repealed) as symbolic, to draw attention to a cause. We rule that the necessity defense is inapplicable to acts of indirect civil disobedience because legal alternatives will never be deemed exhausted when the harm can be mitigated by congressional action.

Concurrence. Perhaps the necessity defense should be grounded more on a concept of what is right and proper under the circumstances rather than on a utilitarian theory alone.

---

c. Defense to murder?

1) **Problem.** The problem is illustrated by *The Queen v. Dudley and Stephens*, *supra*, where a ship went down and the crew on a lifeboat ate the cabin boy in order to survive. It is particularly difficult to determine whether people are really acting out of necessity. If those who take others' lives out of necessity are to be exculpated, then the test for their excuse should be formulated around the conditions that existed at the time they acted and not on conditions that happened long after the act was completed.

2) **General rule.** Criminal acts, done out of necessity, may be excused if the accused can show that they were done to avoid otherwise unavoidable consequences to himself or others he is bound to protect, the results of which would have been irreparable; that no more was done than was absolutely necessary; and that the evil inflicted was not out of proportion to the evil that was threatened. Some courts hold that acts of "economic" necessity are not justified. Almost all courts hold that acts that result in taking another's life are never justified.

   a) For example, most courts would not excuse the defendants in the *Dudley and Stephens* case. However, had such a group taken food that did not belong to them from the ship, this would have been excused.

3) **Model Penal Code.** The Code formulates rules different from those of the majority of jurisdictions:

   a) Conduct the actor believes to be necessary to avoid an evil to himself or another is justifiable, provided:

      (1) The evil sought to be avoided by such conduct is greater than that sought to be prevented by the law defining the crime; and

      (2) The law does not provide for such a situation specifically.

   b) When the actor is reckless or negligent in bringing about the situation requiring a choice of evils or in appraising the necessity for his conduct, the justification afforded by this action is unavailable in a prosecution for any offense for which recklessness or negligence, as the case may be, suffices to establish culpability.

D. PRINCIPLES OF EXCUSE

1. Why Do We Excuse Wrongdoers?

a. **Introduction.** Because punishment for crime is based on the existence of a culpable mental state, some allowance must be made for situations where the mental state is affected to preclude formation of the culpable intent.

b. **Theories of "excuse."** No single theory can explain every use of an "excuse" defense. Under a "causation" theory of excuse, a person should not be held responsible for conduct that was caused by circumstances outside of her control (*e.g.*, mental illness). A "character" theory posits that a person should be excused if one cannot infer the person's bad character from his wrongful conduct (*e.g.*, robbing a bank because a criminal would kill his child if he did not does not suggest bad character). Under a "free choice" or "personhood" theory, a person should not be considered responsible for wrongdoing if she lacked the capacity and/or a fair opportunity freely to choose whether to act in a manner which violates the moral and legal norms of our society (*e.g.*, certain conditions might "harden" one's character and make committing a certain crime appear inevitable).

2. **Duress.**

a. **Statement of the rule.** Acts committed under the immediate threat of death or serious bodily injury, where there is both reasonable cause to believe and actual belief that such harm is threatened, will be excused.

b. **Model Penal Code.**

1) It is an affirmative defense that the actor engaged in conduct because he was "coerced" to do so by the use of, or a threat to use, unlawful force against his person or the person of another, which a person of reasonable firmness in his situation would have been unable to resist.

2) The defense is unavailable if the actor recklessly placed himself in the situation in which it was probable that he would be subjected to duress. It is also unavailable if he was negligent in placing himself in such a situation, whenever negligence suffices for culpability.

c. **Continuing threat to family members--**

United States v. Contento-Pachon, 723 F.2d 691 (9th Cir. 1984).

Facts. Jorge, a Colombian drug trafficker, proposed to Contento-Pachon (D) that he swallow cocaine-filled balloons and fly to the United States. D initially declined to do so, but Jorge threatened the lives of D's family. D did not go to the Colombian police because he believed that they were corrupt. D swallowed 129 balloons of cocaine and flew to the United States. D consented to a stomach x-ray upon his arrival, which revealed the cocaine. At D's trial, the court granted the government's motion to exclude the defenses of duress and necessity because the evidence was insufficient as a matter of law. D appeals.

Issue. May a defendant raise the defense of duress upon a showing that he acted under a continuing and well-grounded threat of serious bodily injury to his family, with no opportunity to escape?

Held. Yes. Judgment reversed.

- The elements of the duress defense are: (i) an immediate threat of death or serious bodily injury; (ii) a well-grounded fear that the threat will be carried out; and (iii) no reasonable opportunity to escape the threatened harm.

- The evidence indicates that D was dealing with a drug trafficker who had taken steps to find out about D's family and who had a large amount of money at stake. Thus, D's fear that his family would be killed was well grounded. Also, D may not have had an opportunity to escape. He would have had to take his family and possessions, leave his job, and go somewhere the drug traffickers could not find him. Alternatively, he would have had to seek protection from police he did not trust. This evidence should go to the jury on a duress defense theory.

- The defense of necessity is inapplicable here, as D's acts were allegedly coerced by human, not physical, forces, and D did not act to promote the general welfare.

Concurrence and dissent. While I agree that the necessity defense is inapplicable here, I also would uphold the trial court's finding that D failed to present sufficient evidence to establish the elements of immediacy and inescapability necessary to prove a duress defense. The record reflects that the initial threat to D and his family took place about three weeks before the flight and threatened only harm that would come if D did not cooperate in the future. The record also shows that during the period between the initial threat and D's swallowing the balloons, D and his family were not physically restrained and could have consulted law enforcement or fled.

---

d. Necessity versus duress--

People v. Unger, 362 N.E.2d 319 (Ill. 1977).

Facts. Unger (D) escaped from a prison's minimum security "honor farm." At his trial for escape, D testified that he had been threatened with homosexual assault, was sexually assaulted, and was threatened with death by one of his attackers, who thought that D had reported the attack. D testified that he was unable to defend himself and that he had intended to turn himself in once he obtained the advice of an attorney. D was convicted of the crime of escape and appealed, arguing that the trial judge instructed the jury to disregard the reasons given for D's escape and failed to instruct the jury of the affirmative defenses of compulsion and necessity. The appellate court reversed, and the state appeals.

Issue. May the defense of necessity be used by a convict who escapes prison?

Held. Yes. Judgment affirmed.

- The defense of compulsion is not the appropriate defense in this case. There was no threat of imminent physical harm together with a demand that D escape. However, the evidence was sufficient to require a jury instruction on the defense of necessity. D was forced to choose between two admitted evils: an illegal escape or a homosexual assault and fear of reprisal.

- In *People v. Lovercamp*, 118 Cal. Rptr. 110 (Cal. Ct. App. 1974), the court allowed the defense of necessity in a similar context. The court set forth five conditions to the defense: (i) specific threat of death, sexual attack, or substantial bodily injury in the immediate future; (ii) no time for a complaint, or a history of futile complaints, to the authorities; (iii) no opportunity or time to resort to the courts; (iv) no force or violence towards innocent persons during the escape; and (v) immediate contact with the proper authorities when the prisoner is safe.

- The above factors are relevant to the propriety of the defense, but they are not all necessary. The absence of one of the conditions does not alone disprove the claim of necessity or preclude instruction on the defense. D was entitled to an appropriate instruction even though he did not promptly contact the authori ties.

---

e. **Defense to murder?--**

People v. Anderson, 50 P.2d 368 (Cal. 2002).

Facts. Anderson (D), Kiern, and others suspected Armstrong of molesting two girls, one of whom was Kiern's daughter. D kidnapped and murdered Armstrong, and later claimed to have killed Armstrong because Kiern threatened to beat him if he failed to do so. Kiern pleaded guilty to Armstrong's second degree murder. D was convicted of first degree murder and kidnapping. D appeals.

Issue.

(i) Does fear for one's own life justify killing an innocent person?

(ii) Can duress reduce murder to manslaughter?

Held. (i) No. (ii) No. Judgment affirmed.

- The rationale for allowing the defense of duress for crimes other than murder is that, for social policy reasons, it is better that the defendant choose to do a lesser evil in order to avoid a greater evil. When a defendant commits murder under duress, however, the resulting harm—the death of an innocent person—is at least as great as the threatened harm—the death of the defendant. The law should require people to choose to resist rather than to kill an innocent person. Moreover, allowing the duress defense for any form of murder would encourage killing. Thus, we conclude that duress is not a defense to any form of murder.

- Section 26 of California's penal code makes duress a defense "unless the crime be punishable with death." D contends that the quoted reference means that the crimes to which duress is not a defense include only those forms of murder that are punishable with death. Today, only first degree murder with special circumstances is so punishable, but first degree murder absent special circumstances was punishable by death when section 26 was adopted and, under common law, all murder was punishable by death. We see no indication that the legislature intended the substantive law of duress to fluctuate with every change in death penalty law or to have abrogated the common law. Moreover, public policy requires deterring, not encouraging, persons to resist rather than kill an innocent person. The legislature, not the court, is in a position to create a new form of voluntary manslaughter to fit the circumstances present in this case.

- Like any killing, killing under duress may or may not be premeditated. Here, the jury found premeditation; in another case, it may not. Unless and until the legislature decides otherwise, a malicious, premeditated killing, even under duress, is first degree murder.

Concurrence and dissent. By referring generally to "a crime not punishable with death," the legislature expressed an intention to incorporate the general body of law relating to capital punishment as it might change over time. It is reasonable to construe the statute as allowing duress as a defense to all but one type of murder, placing it in line with the laws of several other states and countries as well as the Model Penal Code. The majority is concerned that a duress defense to noncapital murder would be used to excuse killings by gang members. However, most gang killings are capital murder because, under state law, it is a special circumstance when a defendant intentionally kills a victim while the defendant is an active participant in a criminal gang and the murder is committed to further the activities of the gang. Furthermore, the defense of duress is not available if a defendant recklessly or intentionally placed himself in a situation where it is reasonable to anticipate pressure to commit crimes. In this case, D did not present sufficient evidence of duress, and he also placed himself in a situation where he should have anticipated pressure to commit acts of violence. Thus, I agree that his conviction should be affirmed.

---

3. **Intoxication.**

   a. **General rule.** Most cases involve voluntary, not involuntary, intoxication. Voluntary intoxication is not a defense to a crime. The idea is that the individual has control over drinking; *i.e.*, he can decide whether he will drink in the first place. He knows the dangers from doing so, and therefore if he drinks he must accept the consequences. However, evidence of drunkenness may be introduced to show that the defendant did not have the requisite intent that is required when specific intent is an element of the crime. For example, murder in the first degree requires premeditation and deliberation; intoxication would perhaps negate this. However, where no specific intent is required (such as for involuntary manslaughter), intoxication would be no defense to the crime.

   b. **Specific intent crimes--**

Commonwealth v. Graves, 334 A.2d 661 (Pa. 1975).

Facts. Graves (D) and two cousins, pursuant to a prior conceived plan, buglarized 75-year-old Patiri's residence and robbed him. In the course of these crimes, Patiri sustained injuries that resulted in his death. At trial, D testified that in the hours before the incident, he consumed at least a quart of wine and took LSD, after which he hallucinated, became unconscious, and suffered limited amnesia. As a result, he claimed, he had no recollection of the incident. A professional psychiatrist rendered his opinion that, at the time of the incident, D's "mind was such that he wasn't able to form the proper conscious intent to take a life, to assault." The trial court sustained an objection to having the doctor testify as to whether D could have consciously formed the specific intent to take or steal and refused to charge the jury that if it found D incapable of forming the intent to commit burglary or robbery because of his intoxication, he could not be guilty of these offenses. D was convicted of first degree murder, robbery, and burglary. D appeals.

Issue. Is the issue of intoxication relevant as to burglary and robbery charges?

Held. Yes. Judgment reversed.

- In making its ruling, the trial court relied on precedent that intoxication is relevant only to the crime of felonious homicide. The rationale was that voluntary intoxication could serve only to lower the degree of a crime, and burglary, robbery, and other crimes contain no analogous degrees of guilt. We now determine that precedent to have been erroneous. Instead, the rule is that voluntary intoxication may be considered in any crime that requires specific intent.

Dissent. The majority's ruling, in effect, will allow voluntary intoxication to serve as an excuse for criminal responsibility. The rationale behind our previous rulings has been that an individual who places himself in a position to have no control over his actions must be held to intend the consequences. Allowing proof of intoxication to lower the degree of a crime does not alter the nature of the crime; *e.g.*, second degree murder is still murder. Allowing it to negate specific intent in crimes with no analogous degrees of guilt permits an individual's voluntary intoxication to serve as a complete exoneration, a result that should not be tolerated.

---

4. Insanity.

a. **Procedural context.** An accused must be competent to stand trial for a criminal trial to proceed. An accused is incompetent unless he has a "sufficient present ability" to communicate with his attorney "with a reasonable degree of rational understanding" and has "a rational as well as factual understanding of the proceedings" against him. [Dusky v. United States, 362 U.S. 402 (1960)] An accused may be found not guilty if, at the time of the crime, he was so impaired by mental illness or retardation that he was "insane." There is a general presumption of sanity, however, so that an accused must affirmatively raise the defense. Many states require the prosecution to prove beyond a reasonable doubt that the accused was sane at the time of the offense, while others require the accused to persuade the jury of his insanity by a preponderance of the evidence. Every jurisdiction has procedures for commitment of an accused found not guilty by reason of insanity. There are several different standards for insanity applied by the various jurisdictions.

b. **Why do we excuse the insane?** In *United States v. Freeman*, 357 F.2d 606 (2d Cir. 1966), the court explained that criminal law is an expression of the moral sense of the community. Over the years, society has recognized that the three functions of the criminal law—rehabilitation, deterrence, and retribution—are not served when one who is mentally incompetent and found guilty is ordered to serve a sentence in prison. Notably, one who is mentally ill is not necessarily insane or mentally incompetent to stand trial.

c. **The tests of insanity--**

State v. Johnson, 399 A.2d 469 (R.I. 1979).

Facts. The facts are not included in the casebook excerpt.

Issue. Should the court abandon the *M'Naghten* test of insanity in favor of a new standard for determining the criminal responsibility of those who claim that they are blameless by reason of mental illness?

Held. Yes.

- Under the *M'Naghten* test, an accused must show that, at the time of committing the act, as a result of his mental illness, he either (i) did not know the nature and quality of his act, or (ii) did not know that the act was wrong. The test has been the subject of frequent criticism. Its emphasis on knowledge of right or wrong abstracts a single element of personality as the sole symptom or manifestation of mental illness. It refuses to recognize volitional or emotional impairments, viewing the cognitive element as the singular cause of conduct—an unrealistic approach. Another common criticism is that it severely limits expert testimony, depriving the jury of a complete picture of the accused's mental condition.

- Under the irresistible impulse or control test, a supplement to *M'Naghten*, a court inquires into both the cognitive and volitional components of the accused's behavior. It permits the acquittal of an accused whose commission of the crime was caused by an insane impulse that controlled his will. It is criticized because, similar to *M'Naghten*'s absolutist view of capacity to know, the irresistible impulse is considered in terms of a complete destruction of the governing power of the mind. The test also suggests that a crime impulsively committed must have been perpetrated in a sudden fit, excluding instances of crimes committed after excessive brooding and melancholy by one who is unable to resist sustained psychotic compulsion or to make any real attempt to control his conduct.

- Under the *Durham* or product test, an accused can be acquitted upon a showing that the crime was the product of a mental illness. The approach was adopted by the Court of Appeals for the District of Columbia in *Durham v. United States*, 214 F.2d 862 (D.C. Cir. 1954) but was later abandoned in *United States v. Brawner*, 471 F.2d 969 (D.C. Cir. 1972). The test had significant deficiencies, as the concept of productivity gave a jury inadequate guidance and it required expert witnesses essentially to usurp the jury's function, deciding whether an act was the product of mental illness.

- Under the Model Penal Code test, an accused may be acquitted by reason of insanity if, because of a mental disease or defect, the accused either (i) lacked substantial capacity to appreciate the criminality of his conduct, or (ii) lacked substantial capacity to conform his conduct to the requirements of law. We adopt a test based on the Model Penal Code approach, as it acknowledges volitional as well as cognitive impairments and uses common vocabulary that will permit a reasonable three-way dialogue among judges and lawyers, medical experts, and the jury.

Comment. The Model Penal Code uses the word "appreciate" rather than "know" to define understanding as more than just a matter of simple cognition.

---

d. ***M'Naghten* and the Model Penal Code in greater detail.**

1) **Knowing/appreciating "wrongfulness" of actions--**

State v. Wilson, 700 A.2d 633 (Conn. 1997).

Facts. Wilson (D) and the victim, Peters, were acquainted through the victim's son, Dirk, with whom D had attended high school. In early 1993, D began to exhibit symptoms of a mental disorder. Specifically, D believed that, in 1981, Dirk had poisoned and hypnotized him to gain control of his thoughts and that Peters was the mastermind of a large organization bent on controlling others' minds. He also believed that Dirk and Peters were responsible for his loss of employment, sexual inadequacy, physical weakness, and other incapacities, as well as the deaths of his mother and several family dogs. Additionally, he blamed the two for his break-up with a former girlfriend. Beginning in February 1993, D informed law enforcement authorities of his beliefs, including his continuing belief that Dirk and Peters were drugging and brainwashing him and others. The police informed him that it was impossible to investigate his allegations. In August 1993, D went to Peters's home, quarreled with him, then shot him numerous times with a gun he had purchased two days earlier. He then went to the police, stated that he had shot Peters because he "had to do it," and gave a sworn statement regarding his beliefs and actions. At trial, D raised mental illness as an affirmative defense. The court refused his proposed instruction that "an accused is not criminally responsible for his offending act if, because of mental disease or defect, he believes that he is morally justified in his conduct—even though he may appreciate that his act is criminal." D was convicted of murder. D appeals.

Issue. Did the trial court err in rejecting D's proposed instruction as to the definition of "wrongfulness?"

Held. Yes. Judgment reversed and case remanded.

- The history of the Model Penal Code indicates that the drafters, by using bracketing to allow state legislatures a choice between the words "wrongfulness" and "criminality," intended that "wrongfulness" convey a moral issue into the test for insanity. We reject the arguments that morality should be defined by purely personal standards or by purely societal standards. We conclude that a defendant does not truly appreciate the wrongfulness of his conduct if a mental disease or defect causes him both to harbor a distorted perception of reality and to believe that, under the circumstances as he honestly perceives them, his actions do not offend societal morality, even though he may also be aware that society, on the basis of the criminal code, does not condone his actions.

- A defendant should not be relieved of criminal liability, however, if his mental illness does not deprive him of substantial capacity to appreciate the boundaries of societal morality and if he elects to transgress those boundaries in pursuit of a delusional personal belief system that he appreciates society itself would not accept.

- Here, D presented sufficient evidence to warrant an instruction such as he proposed.

Concurrence. While I generally agree with the majority, it is my belief that an individual who is mentally ill and, because of that illness, believes that society's rules do not apply to his actions is not capable of appreciating the legal and social import of his actions and, therefore, should not be held criminally responsible. If a defendant's delusional personal belief system is the direct result of his mental illness, the fact that he knows of society's disapproval should not preclude him from successfully pleading an insanity defense.

Dissent. If a defendant recognizes that his conduct is both criminal and wrong in the eyes of society, as murder is, public safety demands that he be held responsible for his actions. I do not agree that it should be a defense that the defendant believes that society did not approve of his conduct only because society failed to appreciate a needed "greater social good" which would come from those same actions.

---

2) Convincing the jury--

State v. Green, 643 S.W.2d 902 (Tenn. Crim. App. 1982).

Facts. Green (D) had been treated for psychiatric problems from the age of seven, when he would fight other children for no reason. He attacked his mother with a knife when he was 12 and began the unusual behavior of not talking to others, laughing hysterically, refusing to bathe, and staying in bed all day and outside all night. At times he was treated with medication. D left his parents' home and lived with various relatives for several months. He continued to exhibit his bizarre behavior. D went to the FBI and told them that someone was directing his mind. D claimed that someone had invented an "ousiograph" machine that could detect this interference. Some time thereafter, a police officer was murdered. A note on the body was addressed to the FBI agent D had contacted and contained nonsensical references to an "ousiograph." D was apprehended after the police contacted the FBI and learned of D's earlier interview. D was charged with the murder but was incompetent to stand trial. After hospitalization, D was deemed competent to stand trial. Despite D's defense of insanity, the jury convicted D of the murder. D appeals, claiming that the overwhelming proof of insanity could not support the verdict.

Issue. May a person be convicted of an offense when the evidence of insanity is overwhelming and is not sufficiently rebutted by the prosecution?

Held. No. Judgment reversed.

- The lay testimony regarding D's strange activity was confirmed by several experts who had evaluated and observed D. These experts unanimously testified that D was insane when he killed the police officer and that D suffered from paranoid schizophrenia. One expert, Dr. Pieper, a neurologist and psychologist, testified that at the time D killed the police officer, D was delusional or hallucinating or both and that he did not understand that what he was doing was wrong.
- The only rebuttal testimony offered by the prosecution was lay testimony to the effect that at certain times shortly after the arrest, D was coherent, polite, and not unusual, but dirty and smelly. This testimony is not inconsistent with the conduct of a paranoid schizophrenic, who can act in a seemingly normal way until someone speaks to him or moves in a way that he perceives as threatening.
- The state's evidence was consistent with the absence of a mental disease, but it was not inconsistent with the presence of the disease, inasmuch as a paranoid schizophrenic can act normally. Thus, the state did not prove beyond a reasonable doubt that D was not suffering from a mental disease.
- The state also failed to prove that D appreciated the wrongfulness of his conduct, although inferences to that effect could be drawn. But even if D did know that what he did was wrong, the evidence does not demonstrate that D could conform to the legal requirements. The only argument that the state made was that because D did not act violently to other police officers, he could control himself. This argument would preclude the insanity defense in any case in which the defendant did not commit an offense against every person, and furthermore it ignores the fact that a paranoid schizophrenic may act normally.
- Because the evidence is insufficient to support the verdict, the conviction must be set aside.

---

5. Diminished Capacity.

a. **Introduction.** In some jurisdictions, evidence of mental illness that does not establish insanity may still be admissible to prove that the defendant did not have the specific intent necessary for the crime charged. Even if the defendant may be aware that her act was wrongful and be able to control it, the mental defect may be characterized as diminished capacity and reduce the extent of criminal liability that would otherwise apply.

b. Insanity and mens rea--

Clark v. Arizona, 126 S.Ct. 2709 (2006).

Facts. Police Officer Moritz responded to complaints about a pickup truck that was playing loud music and circling a residential block. When Officer Moritz pulled over the truck and got out of the patrol car, the truck's driver, Clark (D), shot and killed him. D was charged with first degree murder for intentionally or knowingly killing a law enforcement officer. D was found incompetent to stand trial and was committed to a state mental hospital. Two years later, D was found competent and was ordered to stand trial. At his trial, D claimed a defense based on his undisputed paranoid schizophrenia at the time of the shooting. The prosecution offered circumstantial evidence (*e.g.,* Officer Moritz was in uniform) to show that D knew that Officer Moritz was a law enforcement officer at the time of the shooting. D attempted to use his mental illness to refute the requisite mens rea for the crime. D presented testimony about his paranoid delusions that "aliens" were trying to kill him. His expert concluded that D was incapable of luring the officer, as alleged, or understanding right from wrong. In rebuttal, the prosecution offered expert testimony that D's mental illness did not keep him from appreciating the wrongfulness of his conduct, as shown by his action before and after the shooting (*e.g.,* playing loud music to lure the officer, attempting to evade the police, hiding the gun). The trial court, citing *State v. Mott*, 931 P.2d 1046 (Ariz. 1997), found that D could not rely on evidence bearing on insanity to dispute the mens rea element of the charge. D was convicted of first degree murder and sentenced to life imprisonment without the possibility of release for 25 years. D appealed, claiming a violation of due process, but the court of appeals affirmed. The Supreme Court granted certiorari.

Issues. Is it a violation of due process to prohibit the introduction of evidence of mental illness on the issue of mens rea?

Held. No. Judgment affirmed.

- There are a few categories of evidence with a potential bearing on mens rea. First, there is "observation evidence," which can be presented by either lay or expert witnesses who have observed D's behavior. Second, there is "mental-disease evidence," in the form of expert witness opinions. Finally, there is "capacity evidence." This is also expert opinion evidence. Although *Mott* imposed no restriction on observation evidence, the trial judge here restricted all three types of evidence offered by D for the purpose of showing his inability to form the required mens rea. However, D did not properly object to this improper restriction.

- There is a basic presumption that a defendant is innocent until the government proves beyond a reasonable doubt each element of the offense charged, including the mens rea. However, there is also a presumption of sanity. There are two points where the sanity or capacity presumption may be placed in issue. First, some states allow a defendant to introduce evidence of mental incapacity on the issue of mens rea. This state does not. Second, the presumption of sanity may also be tested by a defense of insanity. The burden falls on the defendant to prove insanity.

- ♦ D argues that it violates due process to restrict him from presenting evidence on an element that must be proven to convict him. However, even relevant evidence may be curtailed if there is good reason. No one denies that a state may place the burden of persuasion on the defendant claiming insanity. Thus, it follows that a state may choose to limit the consideration of mental illness evidence to the insanity defense. The state may wish to avoid a second, less stringent, avenue for exploring capacity, *i.e.,* whether evidence of mental disease created a reasonable doubt as to the issue of mens rea.

- ♦ Finally, evidence in mental disease cases has a potential to mislead jurors. Even in this case, the experts do not agree. Unlike observational evidence bearing on mens rea, capacity evidence consists of judgments that are quite uncertain. It is appropriate for the state to channel such expert testimony to consideration on the insanity defense, where the defendant has the burden of persuasion.

Dissent (Kennedy, Stevens, Ginsburg, JJ.). The issue here is not whether D's mental illness excused him from criminal responsibility, but whether his mental illness, as a factual matter, made him unaware that he was shooting a police officer. D's parents and friends testified that D thought that the people in his town were aliens who were trying to kill him. These claims might not be believable without expert psychiatric testimony confirming experiences of other schizophrenics with similar behaviors. Schizophrenia is a well-documented mental illness, and no one seriously disputes that D was actively psychotic at the time of the crime. The rule applied in this case forces a jury to decide guilt in a fictional world with unexplained behaviors but without mental illness.

---

c. **Model Penal Code.** The Model Penal Code does not limit evidence of mental disease or defect to specific intent crimes, but rather allows it when relevant to the existence of whatever mental state is at issue. The Code also permits evidence of mental disturbance to show that a defendant bears only partial responsibility for his actions, allowing a reduction in a charge of murder to that of manslaughter.

6. **Infancy--**

In re **Devon T.,** 584 A.2d 1287 (Md. Ct. Spec. App. 1991).

Facts. Devon T. (D), 13 years old, was asked by a middle school security guard to empty his pockets. D produced a brown bag containing 20 plastic bags of heroin. D was barely two months under 14, the age at which he would be tried as an adult. D raised the defense of mental incapacity due to infancy. The defense was rejected, and D was convicted of the adult offense of possession of heroin with intent to distribute. D appeals.

Issue. Did the state present sufficient evidence to overcome the presumption of incapacity due to infancy?

Held. Yes. Judgment affirmed.

- To overcome the presumption of D's incapacity due to infancy, the state must produce evidence permitting a reasonable inference that D knew at the time he committed the offense the difference between right and wrong. In short, the infancy defense retains the *M'Naghten* test's exclusive concern with the cognitive element.
- At common law, children possess no cognitive capacity before age seven and all possess it on the day of their 14th birthday. Between those ages, the percentage of children possessing such capacity steadily increases. At his age, a person such as D would most likely possess all cognitive capacity.
- Evidence indicates that, while he later flunked sixth grade, D initially reached sixth grade at 11 years of age, supporting his inclusion in the large majority of his age group. Also, at the hearing before the juvenile master, D acknowledged an understanding of his legal rights and chose to remain silent, a choice from which one might infer some knowledge on D's part of the significance of incrimination. Additionally, the facts show that D had used a house as a "hideout" from which to sell drugs, indicating that he was aware that what he was doing was wrong, and that D bore no needle marks or other indications that he used heroin himself rather than intending to distribute it. Thus, the surrounding circumstances are sufficient to overcome the slight residual weight of the presumption of incapacity due to infancy.

E. NEW DEFENSES

1. Euthanasia--

a. Involuntary euthanasia--

Latimer v. The Queen, 1 S.C.R. 3 (Can. 2001).

Facts. Latimer (D) was convicted of second degree murder for the death of his 12-year-old daughter, Tracy. Tracy suffered from a severe form of cerebral palsy since birth. D had actively participated in his daughter's care. She was quadriplegic and immobile. She was said to have the mental capacity of a four-month-old baby, and it was thought that she was in considerable and constant pain. She had daily seizures and underwent numerous painful surgeries. Despite her severe disabilities, she was not considered terminally ill. Upon learning that the doctors wished to perform yet another painful surgery on his daughter, D decided to take her life. D put Tracy in his truck and inserted a hose connected to the truck's exhaust pipe into the cab. Tracy died from the carbon monoxide. D appeals his conviction.

Issue. Should the jury have been entitled to consider the defense of necessity?

Held. No. Appeal dismissed.

- ♦ Three elements are required for the defense of necessity. First, there must be an urgent situation of clear and imminent peril. Second, there must be no reasonable legal alternative to disobeying the law. Finally, there must be proportionality between the harm inflicted and the harm avoided.

- ♦ Here, there is no air of reality to the three requirements of necessity. There was no emergency involved with the surgery; rather this was part of a long-standing state of affairs. Second, D clearly had a reasonable legal alternative to killing his daughter. He could have simply continued on, in what was unquestionably a difficult situation, helping Tracy in any way possible. Third, the harm in this case, ending a life, was immeasurably more serious than the pain resulting from the operation that D sought to avoid. Killing a person to relieve suffering from a non-life-threatening medical condition is not a proportional response.

---

b. Voluntary euthanasia--

People v. Kevorkian, 639 N.W.2d 291 (Mich. Ct. App. 2001).

Facts. Dr. Kevorkian (D) administered a lethal injection to Youk, who was suffering from ALS (Lou Gehrig's disease). Youk indicated his consent on videotape and in writing. The medical examiner listed the manner of death as homicide and the cause of death the lethal injection, finding that the ALS was not an underlying cause of Youk's death and did not contribute to his death in any way. D was convicted of second degree murder and sentenced to 10 to 25 years. D appeals.

Issue. Is there a constitutional right to commit euthanasia?

Held. No. Judgment affirmed.

- ♦ D does not assert that he acted in furtherance of Youk's right to refuse life-sustaining medical treatment or that he used medicine to relieve Youk's pain or discomfort even though it hastened Youk's death, actions which might be protected constitutionally or through state legislation. D also does not contend that he assisted Youk's suicide by providing the physical means by which Youk committed suicide, which in any event is prohibited by Michigan law. Instead, he asserts that the right to be free from unbearable pain and suffering due to a medical condition is inherently part of the liberty interest secured by the Fourteenth Amendment Due Process Clause and its Michigan counterpart, and he should not be prosecuted for his actions in aiding Youk's assertion of his constitutional right.

- No court of last resort has recognized the right to privacy to include a right to commit euthanasia so that an individual can be freed from intolerable and irremediable suffering. In *Washington v. Glucksberg*, 521 U.S. 702 (1997), the United States Supreme Court held that the asserted "right" to assisted suicide is not a protected fundamental liberty interest and referred to the "slippery slope" argument that permitting assisted suicide might someday lead to the use of voluntary or even involuntary euthanasia. We are unwilling to expand the right to privacy in such a way that would begin the slide down this slippery slope.
- If society were to recognize a right to be free from intolerable and irremediable suffering, it should be the result of the legislative process. Expanding the right to privacy as D suggests would, to a great extent, place the matter outside the arena of public debate and legislative action.
- Finally, we observe that expanding the right of privacy to include euthanasia would inevitably involve the judiciary in deciding questions that are beyond its capacity, such as how much pain is necessary before suffering becomes "intolerable."

---

2. Addiction/Alcoholism Defense.

a. Drug addiction--

Robinson v. California, 370 U.S. 660 (1962).

Facts. Robinson (D) was prosecuted for being "addicted to the use of narcotics." The evidence showed that D had scar tissue, needle marks, and discoloration typical of frequent narcotics users. The jury was instructed that D could be convicted if it found that D was either of the "status" or had committed the "act" proscribed by the statute. D was found guilty and appeals.

Issue. May a state criminalize mere status as a narcotics addict?

Held. No. Judgment reversed.

- A state has broad power to regulate narcotics traffic. It can even involuntarily confine addicts for compulsory medical treatment. However, a disease is not a criminal offense. D may have been convicted under the statute without ever having used or possessed narcotics within the state and without ever having done any antisocial act there. Criminal punishment for affliction with a disease is cruel and unusual. A drug addict is a sick person, not a criminal.

Concurrence (Douglas, J.). An addict is sick and we should not allow sickness to be treated as a crime. Civil commitment would protect society just as well.

Concurrence (Harlan, J.). Drug addiction may be something other than an illness and therefore subject to criminal sanctions, but this statute allows conviction for the bare desire to do a criminal act, *e.g.*, D's compelling propensity to use narcotics.

Dissent (White, J.). The court has made it impossible for the state to deal with defendants who continually use narcotics where the state cannot prove the precise location of use.

---

b. Alcoholism--

Powell v. Texas, 392 U.S. 514 (1968).

Facts. Powell (D) was arrested and charged with being found intoxicated in a public place. He was found guilty and fined $50. On appeal, the court ruled that chronic alcoholism, from which D suffered, was not a defense to the charge. D appeals.

Issue. May a person be criminally liable for merely being in a public place while intoxicated?

Held. Yes. Judgment affirmed.

- Alcoholism presents a serious public problem. The evidence indicates that there is no known generally effective method for treating alcoholism. Use of the criminal law to incarcerate public drunks affords an opportunity to sober up. Because penal incarceration has stringent time limits, it is probably preferable to an unlimited civil commitment when no treatment is available. The uncertainty of any deterrent effect of the criminal statute does not make the statute unconstitutional.

- In *Robinson v. California, supra*, the court held that a statute making it a crime to "be addicted to the use of narcotics" inflicted cruel and unusual punishment because it punished the person's condition. The statute here materially differs because it punishes not chronic alcoholism but public drunkenness. *Robinson* requires some actus reus before criminal penalties may be inflicted. D did commit an illegal act.

Concurrence (Black, Harlan, JJ.). Punishment of chronic alcoholics can be justified in terms of deterrence because it gives the potential alcoholic an incentive to control his drinking and may strengthen the chronic alcoholic's incentive to control the frequency and location of his drinking. Also, jailing the chronic alcoholic is therapeutic because he is given food, clothing, and shelter while he sobers up, and it protects others because it gets him off the streets where he may cause harm. Moreover, *Robinson* was limited to situations where no act was involved and where the mental element is not simply one part of the crime, but all of it. To expand the boundaries of *Robinson* would render the states powerless to punish any conduct that results from a compulsion.

Concurrence (White, J.). If it is not a crime to have an irresistible compulsion to use drugs, it should not be a crime to yield to the compulsion. Here, however, D did not have an irresistible compulsion to be in the public area. He could have taken precautions against being drunk in public.

Dissent (Fortas, Douglas, Brennan, Stewart, JJ.). The Constitution forbids infliction of criminal penalties upon a person for being in a condition he is powerless to change. D was convicted only because he was in a condition that he had no capacity to change or avoid.

---

3. **"Rotten Social Background" Defense.** There is some debate as to whether a person can validly assert a defense that he should be acquitted of a crime because his behavioral controls were undermined by his social and economic background.

4. **Cultural Defense--**

State v. Kargar, 679 A.2d 81 (Me. 1996).

Facts. Kargar (D), an Afghani refugee, was reported to police after a neighbor witnessed D kissing his infant son's penis. A photo album also included a picture of D kissing his son's penis. D explained to police, and ultimately proffered testimony of many Afghani people in support of his *de minimis* motion to dismiss, that such an action is accepted as common practice in his culture to show parental love for a young son. He also provided evidence that the practice does not involve sexual feelings and that, in fact, Islamic law imposes the death penalty for any sexual activity between an adult and a child. The state did not present witnesses during the hearing on D's motion to dismiss. The court denied D's motion and convicted him of two counts of gross sexual assault, although it imposed an entirely suspended sentence. D appeals.

Issue. Were D's culture, alleged lack of harm, and innocent state of mind relevant to the determination of D's guilt?

Held. Yes. Judgment reversed.

- Maine has a *de minimis* statute that requires courts to take into consideration the nature of a defendant's conduct and the attendant circumstances. Some circumstances worthy of cognizance are: the background, experience, and character of the defendant which may indicate whether he ought to have known that his conduct was illegal; the circumstances concerning the offense; the resulting harm or evil, if any, caused by the defendant's conduct; the probable impact of the violation upon the community; and any other data which may reveal the nature and degree of the defendant's culpability.

- Here, the court denied D's motion without considering the full range of relevant factors. The court improperly focused on whether the conduct met the definition of the gross sexual assault statute rather than on whether the admittedly criminal conduct was envisioned by the legislature when it defined the crime. A review of legislative history reveals that it intended that for this type of act to be criminal it must be done for the purpose of either sexual gratification or to cause bodily injury or offensive physical contact. The evidence presented at the *de minimis* hearing supports the conclusion that there was nothing sexual about D's conduct. Furthermore, dismissing this case would pose little harm to the community.

Comment. Most states have not enacted a *de minimis* statute, so a person such as D would have to hope that charges would not be brought against him or would be dropped, that a jury would be willing to nullify the law, or that, if convicted, a judge would consider his culture in determining an appropriate sentence.

X. INCHOATE OFFENSES

A. ATTEMPT

1. **Introduction.** Both at common law and under most modern statutes, it is a crime to attempt the commission of any felony or misdemeanor. Merely taking steps toward the completion of a crime, if done with the requisite intent, may be a crime itself. Attempt consists of: (i) a specific intent to commit a crime; and (ii) an act in furtherance of that intent, which goes far enough toward completion of the crime.

2. **Mens Rea.** The mens rea of attempt has two components: (i) the intent to commit the acts or cause the result constituting the crime; and (ii) the intent necessary for the completed crime. Therefore, if the crime allegedly attempted requires specific intent, such as burglary, the defendant must have had the specific intent to commit burglary.

   a. **Specific intent--**

People v. Gentry, 510 N.E.2d 963 (Ill. App. Ct. 1987).

Facts. Gentry (D) and his girlfriend, Ruby Hill, began arguing after drinking together all afternoon. D spilled gasoline on Hill, and the gasoline ignited when she went near a stove in the kitchen. D smothered the flames with a coat, but Hill had already been severely burned. D was convicted of attempt murder and appeals.

Issue. Is the specific intent to kill a pivotal element of the crime of attempt murder?

Held. Yes. Judgment reversed and case remanded.

- The trial court instructed the jury on attempt by saying: "A person commits the offense of murder when he, with intent to commit the offense of murder, does any act which constitutes a substantial step toward the commission of the offense of murder. The offense need not have been completed."

- The court then instructed the jury on the four alternative states of mind that make a person culpable for murder: (i) intent to kill, (ii) intent to cause great bodily harm, (iii) knowledge that such acts will cause death, or (iv) knowledge that such acts create the strong probability of death or great bodily harm.

- D contends that the inclusion of the four alternative states of mind in the definition of murder was erroneous because the crime of attempt murder requires a specific intent to kill.

- We agree and find that the specific intent to kill is a necessary element of the crime of attempt murder. The jury was misinstructed.

---

b. **Attempted felony murder--**

Bruce v. State, 566 A.2d 103 (Md. 1989).

Facts. Bruce (D) and two other men went into a shoe store, where D ordered the owner, Tensor, to open the cash register. When D saw that the cash register was empty, he became angry. At trial, Tensor testified that D held a gun to his head and told Tensor that he was going to kill him. While trying to get out of the way, Tensor bumped into D and was shot. Tensor was subsequently hospitalized for a gunshot wound to his stomach. D was found guilty of attempted first degree felony murder, robbery with a deadly weapon, and two handgun charges. D appeals the attempted felony murder verdict.

Issue. Is attempted felony murder a crime in the state of Maryland?

Held. No. Judgment reversed and case remanded.

- The felony murder statute in Maryland provides that all murder committed in the perpetration of, or attempt to perpetrate, certain designated felonies, of which robbery is one, is also murder in the first degree.
- To convict a person under the felony murder statute, the state is required to prove a specific intent to commit the underlying felony; it is not necessary to prove a specific intent to kill.
- Under Maryland law, attempt is a specific intent crime. Because a conviction for felony murder requires no specific intent to kill, and because a criminal attempt is a specific intent crime, attempted felony murder is not a crime in Maryland.

---

3. **Actus Reus.**

a. **Introduction.** The actus reus of attempt is an act that progresses sufficiently toward the commission of the offense. Whether a defendant has done enough in furtherance of his intent to have committed attempt is not subject to any precise rule. Various approaches have been used.

b. **Traditional approach.** Some courts hold that the defendant's acts must have gone beyond mere "preparation" into the zone of "perpetration."

However, because there is much confusion as to when preparation ends and perpetration begins, this formula is not always useful.

c. **Alternative approaches.** The difficulty in applying the traditional approach in a consistent and fair manner has led some courts to apply alternative analyses.

1) **The physical proximity doctrine.** Some have suggested that the defendant's conduct must be physically proximate to the intended crime, the focus being on what remains to be done as opposed to what was already done.

2) **The dangerous proximity doctrine.** Under this doctrine, attempt may be found when the distance between the defendant's actions and the consummated crime is dangerously close.

3) **The indispensable element test.** An alternative test requires that the defendant go far enough to have obtained control over all factors that are indispensable to the commission of the crime. Thus, nothing must be left undone that would prevent the defendant from committing the crime.

4) **The probable desistance test.** Another approach is to find an attempt only when the act is such that in the ordinary course of events it would lead to completion of the crime in the absence of intervening outside factors. Thus, the emphasis here is upon the likelihood that the defendant would cease his efforts to commit the crime, given the actions he has already committed.

5) **Abnormal step approach.** Still another approach is to find attempt when the defendant took a step toward crime that goes beyond the point where a normal citizen would think better of his conduct and stop.

6) **The res ipsa loquitur or unequivocality test.** This variation suggests that an act amounts to attempt only if—when considered alone—it firmly shows the actor's intent to commit the crime. Hence, the accused's behavior is considered without reference to other evidence that may demonstrate criminal intent (such as a confession); the act relied upon to constitute attempt must "speak for itself" in establishing intent.

7) **Model Penal Code approach.** Departing from the approaches considered above, the Model Penal Code would require an act constituting a "substantial step" in the course of conduct intended to result in the crime. In addition, the conduct must be "strongly corroborative" of the defendant's criminal purpose, although it need not establish purpose by itself.

8) **Substantial step.** In *United States v. Mandujano*, 499 F.2d 370 (5th Cir. 1974), the court noted that there is no legislative history explaining what "attempt" means in 21 U.S.C.A. section 846, which addresses penalties for attempt and conspiracy involving drugs. The court discussed the difficulty of distinguishing attempt from mere preparation and said that, for attempt, there must have been a substantial step toward commission of the crime, which means that an appreciable fragment of the crime must have been committed.

d. **Distinguishing preparation from perpetration: the tests at work.**

1) **Overt act--**

Commonwealth v. Peaslee, 59 N.E.2d 55 (Mass. 1901).

Facts. Peaslee (D) placed combustible items in a building in such a way that, if they were lighted, they would have set fire to the building and its contents. He placed a candle nearby that was required to ignite the fire. He then left the building and attempted to solicit an employee of his to ignite the fire. The employee refused. D later drove the employee to within a quarter of a mile from the building, but D then changed his mind and drove away. D was indicted for an attempt to burn a building with intent to injure the insurers. D's motion to quash the indictment and request for a directed verdict were denied. D appeals.

Issue. Was D guilty of attempt?

Held. No. Judgment reversed.

- The issue is whether D's acts came near enough to the accomplishment of the substantive offense to be punishable.

- The first steps toward accomplishing an offense do not constitute an attempt if further acts are necessary. "Attempt" suggests an act seemingly sufficient to accomplish the end. Whether preparation amounts to an attempt is a question of degree, and the degree of proximity that is sufficient to constitute attempt varies with the circumstances. However, if a crime is thwarted by police intervention or the defendant's mistake of judgment after the defendant has set in motion forces that would bring about the crime, the defendant is punishable for attempt.

- In this case, D's preparation, without any present intent to set the fire, was too remote to be considered an attempt. On the other hand, D's solicitation of someone else to set the fire could be seen as an overt act of attempt. However, the indictment did not allege D's solicitation of his employee and is, therefore, insufficient to convict D of attempt.

2) Dangerous proximity test--

People v. Rizzo, 158 N.E. 888 (N.Y. 1927).

Facts. Rizzo (D) and three other men planned to rob Rao of a payroll valued at about $1,200, which Rao was to carry from the bank for the United Lathing Company. Two of the men with D had firearms. The four men started out in a car, looking for Rao. D was to point him out to the others, who were to do the actual holding up. The four drove around looking for Rao, and at some point were watched and followed by two police officers. At a United Lathing Company building, when Rizzo jumped out of the car and ran into the building, all four were arrested. D was taken out from the building where he had been hiding. Rao was not in the building, and no one had been identified by D. D was convicted of an attempt to commit robbery in the first degree. D appeals.

Issue. Is a defendant guilty of attempt to commit robbery in the first degree if he never found the person he intended to rob?

Held. No. Judgment reversed and case remanded.

- There is no doubt that D had the intention to commit the robbery. However, there must be a "dangerous proximity to success" in order to convict a defendant of attempt; the acts must come very near to the accomplishment of the crime.

- To commit the robbery, the money must have been taken from Rao through force, violence, or fear; D was still looking for Rao when the police arrested him. No attempt could be made to rob Rao until he at least came in sight. D had planned to commit a crime and was looking for an opportunity to commit it, but the opportunity never came.

3) Unequivocal act--

People v. Miller, 42 P.2d 308 (Cal. 1935).

Facts. After threatening to kill Albert Jeans, Miller (D) went to a field where Jeans was working. D walked toward Jeans, stopped, and appeared to be loading a rifle he was carrying. D did not lift his gun to take aim, but Jeans saw him and ran away. D walked toward Ginochio, Jeans's employer and the constable of the town. Ginochio took the loaded gun from D, who did not resist. At trial, D was found guilty of attempt to commit murder. D appeals.

Issue. Do the steps taken by D constitute an unequivocal act constituting attempt?

Held. No. Judgment reversed.

- To constitute attempt, there must be some direct act toward consummation of the intended crime, as distinguished from mere preparation. The act must be unequivocal in order to determine with certainty what the defendant intended.

- In this case, no one could say with certainty whether D intended to kill Jeans or whether he intended to demand that the constable arrest Jeans. Thus, D's acts do not constitute an attempt to commit murder.

---

4) **Substantial step--**

State v. Reeves, 916 S.W.2d 909 (Tenn. 1996).

Facts. Tracie Reeves (D) and her classmate, Molly Coffman, 12-year-old students, agreed to kill their homeroom teacher. The girls planned to place rat poison in their teacher's drink. They also agreed to steal the teacher's car and drive to the Smoky Mountains. D contacted a high school student to tell him of the plan and ask his assistance in driving the car, but he refused. The next day, Coffman put rat poison in her purse and proceeded to school. On the bus ride to school, Coffman told the plan to another student. Upon arriving at school, the other student told her teacher of the girls' plan, and her teacher told the principal. When the girls' teacher entered her classroom, she found them leaning over her desk. The girls then giggled and ran back to their seats. The teacher found a purse lying next to her coffee cup on top of the desk. A short time later, the principal called Coffman to her office, and rat poison was found in Coffman's purse. D and Coffman were designated delinquents after a jury found that they had attempted to commit second degree murder. D appeals.

Issue. Did D's acts constitute a substantial step toward the commission of murder?

Held. Yes. Judgment affirmed.

- Before the 1989 codification of Tennessee's criminal attempt statute, criminal attempt was judicially defined. One of the elements of criminal attempt was an overt act toward the commission of the intended crime. Tennessee courts construed the term "overt act" very narrowly and drew a sharp distinction between "mere preparation" and an "overt act." In contrast, under the 1989 criminal attempt statute, criminal attempt includes conduct that "constitutes a substantial step toward the commission of the offense" if the defendant's "entire course of action is corroborative of the intent to commit the offense." [Tenn. Code Ann. §39-12-101]

- The state argues that the Tennessee statute closely follows the Model Penal Code section 5.01(2)(e) and (f), which provides that the following examples of conduct, if strongly corroborative of the defendant's criminal purpose, will be held to be sufficient as a matter of law: (i) "possession of materials to be employed in the commission of the crime, which are specifically designed for such unlawful use or which can serve no lawful purpose of the actor under the circumstances;" and (ii) "possession, collection or fabrication of materials to be employed in the commission of the crime, at or near the place contemplated for its commission, where such possession, collection or fabrication serves no lawful purpose of the actor under the circumstances."

- D counters that the Tennessee legislature did not include the examples stated in the Model Penal Code in the revised state statute and that this shows that they intended to retain a sharp distinction between "mere preparation" and the "act itself." D argues that her conviction must be reversed because her actions constitute "mere preparation" under the rules stated in *Dupuy v. State,* 325 S.W.2d 238 (1959). Under *Dupuy*, no criminal responsibility would have attached unless the poison had been placed in the teacher's cup.

- *Dupuy*, which was decided before the enactment of our criminal attempt statute, has been criticized because of the difficulty of distinguishing between mere preparation and the act itself. Furthermore, the test for criminal intent under *Dupuy* is inconsistent with our criminal attempt statute. Failing to attach criminal responsibility until a person is on the brink of consummating a crime endangers the public and undercuts the goal of preventing inchoate crimes from becoming full-blown crimes.

- We hold that when a person possesses materials to be used in the commission of a crime, at or near the scene of the crime, and the possession of those materials serves no lawful purpose, the jury may find that the person has taken a "substantial step" toward commission of the crime.

Concurrence and dissent. The "course of action" of these girls was not "strongly corroborative" of intent to commit second degree murder, and the evidence was insufficient as a matter of law. While I concur with the majority's abandonment of *Dupuy v. State*, I dissent from the majority's conclusion.

---

e. Punishing pre-attempt conduct--

United States v. Alkhabaz, 104 F.3d 1492 (6th Cir. 1997).

Facts. Alkhabaz (D) and Gonda exchanged e-mail messages that expressed a sexual interest in violence against women and girls. D also posted on the Internet fictional stories that involved the abduction, rape, torture, mutilation, and murder of women and young girls. One story that D posted described the torture, rape, and murder of a young woman who shared the name of one of his classmates at the University of Michigan. Subsequently, D was arrested on a criminal complaint alleging violations of 18 U.S.C. section 875(c), which prohibits interstate communications containing threats to kidnap or injure another person. The district court quashed the indictment. The United States appeals.

Issue. Does 18 U.S.C. section 875(c) prohibit the communication of fictional stories describing violence against women?

Held. No. Judgment affirmed.

- ♦ To support a conviction under section 875(c), the government must prove three elements: (i) there was a transmission in interstate or foreign commerce; (ii) there was a communication containing a threat; and (iii) the threat was to injure or kidnap another person. The second element raises the question of what is meant by a communication containing a threat.
- ♦ A communication does not contain a threat unless the communication is used to further some goal through the use of intimidation. The communication must be such that a reasonable person would take the statement as a serious expression of an intention to inflict bodily harm and would perceive such expression as being communicated to effect some change or achieve some goal through intimidation.
- ♦ In this case, no reasonable person would perceive D's communications as being conveyed to effect some change or achieve some goal through intimidation. Thus, they did not constitute "communications containing a threat." D and Gonda sent e-mail messages to each other to foster a friendship based on shared sexual fantasies.

Dissent. Section 875(c) clearly relates to communication that contains any threat to kidnap or physically injure any person and that is made for any or no reason. The communications are not limited to those directed to identified individuals and intended to effect some change or goal.

---

4. Special Defenses.

a. **Impossibility.** An accused may assert as a defense that he could not have succeeded in his attempt due to some type of impossibility. Courts have differed on the effect of a showing that successful completion of the planned crime was impossible.

1) **Factual impossibility.** Factual impossibility exists where the defendant intends to commit a crime and does everything he can to do so, but because of factors of which he is unaware, it is impos-

sible for him to bring about the intended result. Factual impossibility is, by general agreement, no defense to an attempt charge. Thus, for example, a defendant's efforts to steal money from a victim's pocket would support a conviction for attempted theft, even though, unbeknownst to the defendant, the pocket was empty. The defendant did everything he could do to effect the consummation of the crime and failed only because of circumstances not previously apparent to him.

2) **Legal impossibility.** Legal impossibility arises when the accused intends to commit a crime, but his conduct, even if successfully completed, would not constitute a crime (*e.g.*, shooting a stuffed deer out of season believing it to be a real deer). Whether legal impossibility is or should be a defense to attempt is subject to a split of authority, although traditionally courts have held that it is a defense.

3) **Inherent impossibility.** If the accused's conduct obviously could not produce the criminal object, no criminal liability attaches. Thus, one who attempts to kill by voodoo cannot be convicted for attempted murder no matter how far he has progressed in his efforts, because it is inherently impossible to achieve the criminal objective by the means employed.

4) **Hybrid legal impossibility--**

People v. Thousand, 631 N.W.2d 694 (Mich. 2001).

Facts. Officer Liczbinski was conducting an undercover investigation for the county's Internet Crimes Bureau in which he posed as a female minor ("Bekka") and logged onto chat rooms. Bekka was approached by Thousand (D) in a chat room, and the two engaged in several conversations during which Bekka repeatedly indicated that she was 14 years old. Eventually the online conversations became sexually explicit. At one point, D e-mailed the undercover officer a photograph of his genitals and asked Bekka to meet him at a McDonald's and come back to his house for sex. Officers waited for D at the McDonald's and apprehended him when he came in looking for Bekka. D was charged with attempted distribution of obscene material to a minor. D brought a motion to quash, arguing that the existence of a child victim was an element of the charge and, as no child was involved, he could not be found guilty. The court agreed and dismissed the charge on the basis of legal impossibility. The appellate court affirmed. The state appeals.

Issue. Did the trial court err in dismissing the charge on the basis of legal impossibility?

Held. Yes. Judgment reversed in part, affirmed in part, and case remanded.

- Legal impossibility applies when a person engages in conduct that he believes is criminal, but which is not actually prohibited by law. "Hybrid" legal impossibility exists when the perpetrator's goal was illegal, but commission of the offense was impossible due to a factual mistake regarding the legal status of some factor relevant to his conduct. Virtually any example of hybrid legal impossibility may be viewed as an example of factual impossibility. Factual impossibility has apparently never been recognized as a defense to a charge of attempt.

- In this case, D clearly could not be convicted of the substantive crime of distributing obscene materials to a minor because no minor was actually involved. However, he did attempt to distribute obscene materials to someone he believed to be a minor.

- Under our state statute, an "attempt" consists of: (i) an attempt to commit an offense prohibited by law, and (ii) any act towards the commission of the intended offense. Our state law carves out no exception for a defendant who, acting with the requisite criminal intent to commit an offense prohibited by law, takes action toward the commission of that offense even though he acted under a misconception.

- D is not charged with the substantive crime of distributing obscene material to a minor; he is charged with attempt. The nonexistence of a minor victim is not a defense to the attempt charge. The trial court erred in dismissing the charge solely on the basis of legal impossibility.

Dissent. I disagree that legal impossibility has never been adopted by Michigan courts. There is ample evidence that "legal impossibility" is a viable defense. Examination of the language of the attempt statute leads to a reasonable inference that the legislature did not intend to punish conduct that a mistake of legal fact renders unprohibited. The attempt statute codified the common law, which recognized "legal impossibility" as a defense to attempt. If an element of the offense cannot be established, an accused cannot be found guilty of the prohibited act. The underlying offense in this case, disseminating obscene material to a minor, requires a minor recipient. Because the dissemination was not to a minor, it is legally impossible for the defendant to have committed the prohibited act.

---

b. Abandonment--

Commonwealth v. McCloskey, 341 A.2d 500 (Pa. Super. Ct. 1975).

Facts. McCloskey (D) was serving a prison sentence of one to three years for larceny. One night while working his shift in the boiler room, D left the boiler room, carrying a bag of civilian clothing. D cut a piece of barbed wire and scaled a fence within the prison walls that led to the recreation yard and then to the prison wall. D went only as far as the yard before giving up his plan to escape and returning to work in the boiler room. Later, D voluntarily told a guard supervisor that he had contemplated a prison break but changed his mind because he felt that he had already shamed his family enough. At trial, D was convicted for an attempted prison breach. D appeals.

Issue. Do preparatory acts that are voluntarily abandoned before a crime is committed constitute an attempt?

Held. No. Judgment vacated.

- Because D was still within the prison, only contemplating a prison breach, he had not yet attempted the act. D was in a position to abandon the criminal offense voluntarily, and he exonerated himself from criminal responsibility.

Concurrence. Although I agree with the majority that D's conviction should not stand, I disagree with the majority's conclusion that D's acts before his decision to abandon his escape were insufficient to constitute an attempt. If D had been apprehended by the guards immediately after he had cut the barbed wire and crossed the inner fence, his conviction would have been affirmed. The majority has erred in acknowledging D's abandonment by characterizing his conduct as preparatory. Our Crimes Code recognizes that voluntary abandonment is a complete defense to a charge of attempt. Although D was charged under our old penal code, which did not address whether voluntary abandonment was a defense to an attempt charge, this court long ago recognized voluntary abandonment as an affirmative defense to the crime of attempt. Furthermore, the knowledge that voluntary abandonment exonerates a person from criminal liability provides a motive to stop before completing the crime.

B. ASSAULT

At one time, assault was typically defined as an unlawful attempt to inflict bodily injury on another, coupled with a present ability to succeed. An assault required greater proximity to the completed offense than did an attempt to commit the offense. Thus, some acts that constituted a criminal attempt would not satisfy the proximity requirement of assault. By the time the Model Code was drafted, the majority of jurisdictions had expanded the assault offense so that it encompassed both an attempt to commit a battery and an intentional creation, other than by mere words, of a reasonable apprehension of imminent bodily harm. Although the Model Code definition of assault has abandoned the requirement of greater proximity to success, it includes completed offenses as well as attempts.

C. SOLICITATION

1. **Common Law.** At common law, it was a misdemeanor to counsel, incite, or

induce another to commit or to join in the commission of any offense, whether that offense was a felony or a misdemeanor.

2. **Modern Statutes.** Some states have no statute making solicitation a crime, and states that do have solicitation statutes vary considerably in their coverage. Some limit the crime to solicitation of certain serious offenses, such as murder, rape, kidnapping, and robbery. Other jurisdictions have statutes that cover solicitation of all crimes. Statutory treatment of solicitation also varies significantly. In some jurisdictions, the punishment for solicitation is the same as that for the solicited offense. In other jurisdictions, solicitation is punishable to a lesser degree than the completed offense.

3. **Mens Rea.** The crime of solicitation requires a showing that the defendant acted volitionally and with the intent or purpose of causing the person solicited to commit the crime.

4. **Actus Reus.** The only act required for the commission of the crime is the counseling, inciting, or inducing of another to commit the offense. The crime of solicitation is complete upon the performance of this act.

5. **Comparison with Attempt.** Unlike solicitation, attempt requires that the defendant have progressed far enough in his criminal scheme to have gone beyond mere preparation. Generally, a person who does the bare minimum that suffices for solicitation will not be liable for attempt. At the same time, however, if the defendant continues to assist the person solicited, he may well incur liability as a party to an attempt to commit the crime.

6. **Solicitor's Culpability.** One reason why the punishment for solicitation varies in different jurisdictions is because of differing views of the solicitor's culpability. Some consider a solicitor to be less of a menace because he manifests an unwillingness to commit the actual crime himself. Others believe that a solicitor is more dangerous because he is the mastermind behind the crime. In *State v. Mann*, 345 S.E.2d 365 (N.C. 1986), the court expressed this latter view when it described the solicitor's approach to crime. The court went on to say that a solicitation, "an attempt to conspire," may be more dangerous than an attempt, and a solicitor may be more dangerous than a conspirator, who may merely agree to a criminal plan. "[T]he solicitor plans, schemes, suggests, encourages, and incites the solicitation. Further, the solicitor is morally more culpable than a conspirator; he keeps himself from being at risk, hiding behind the actor."

7. **Communication Required--**

State v. Cotton, 790 P.2d 1050 (N.M. Ct. App. 1990).

Facts. Cotton (D) was charged with multiple counts of criminal sexual conduct with a minor, stemming from events that involved his 14-year-old stepdaughter. While in prison awaiting trial on these charges, D wrote several letters to his wife strategizing a plan to defend against the criminal charges. In two letters, he asked his wife to help him persuade his stepdaughter not to testify against him. These two letters were never received by his wife, but were instead confiscated by law enforcement authorities. D was convicted of two counts of criminal solicitation. D appeals.

Issue. Can an uncommunicated solicitation to commit a crime constitute the offense of criminal solicitation?

Held. No. Judgment reversed and case remanded.

- ♦ The state reasons that even in the absence of evidence indicating that the communications were received, D is still guilty of writing the letters and attempting to send them, and he had the specific intent to solicit the commission of a crime. We disagree.

- ♦ Our state statute defining criminal solicitation adopts, in part, language of the Model Penal Code. However, our statute omits the portion of the Model Penal Code subsection that states that an uncommunicated solicitation to commit a crime may constitute criminal solicitation. This omission indicates an implicit legislative intent that the offense of solicitation requires some form of actual communication. This does not mean that the solicitor could not be prosecuted for an attempt to solicit.

D. CONSPIRACY

1. **General Principles.** Conspiracy is an agreement between two or more persons to do an unlawful act or to do a lawful act in an unlawful manner. At common law, conspiracy was a misdemeanor, and if the substantive crime was actually committed, then the misdemeanor merged into the actual crime committed. Today, however, conspiracy is punishable as a separate and distinct crime. "The crime is complete upon formation of the agreement." [People v. Carter, 330 N.W.2d 314 (Mich. 1982)] Therefore, the defendant may be prosecuted for both the conspiracy and the substantive crime, and the sentences may be added together on conviction.

2. **No Direct Participation Necessary--**

Pinkerton v. United States, 328 U.S. 640 (1946).

Facts. Daniel and Walter Pinkerton (Ds) were prosecuted for conspiracy to commit violations of the Internal Revenue Code and for substantive violations. Only Walter committed the actual violations, but both brothers were convicted of conspiracy and certain of the substantive violations. Daniel appeals.

Issue. May a conspirator be convicted of committing the offense intended by the conspiracy although he had no direct participation in the actual commission?

Held. Yes. Judgment affirmed.

- Once Daniel conspired with Walter, he became equally responsible with Walter for acts done in furtherance of the conspiracy. The conspiracy was continuous. There is no evidence that Daniel withdrew from the conspiracy before Walter acted. The criminal intent necessary was established by the formation of the conspiracy. Thus, Daniel was properly convicted of the substantive offenses.

Dissent (Rutledge, J.). All the government proved was that Daniel had, in the past, conspired with Walter to commit violations similar to those committed in this case. There is no evidence that Daniel conspired to commit the particular acts that Walter committed here. Daniel was even in prison when Walter committed some of the acts.

---

3. **Relationship of the Law of Conspiracy to the Law of Evidence.** It is difficult to understand the law of conspiracy unless one understands the law of evidence.

   a. **Hearsay rule.** The hearsay rule requires that one testify only about those things that he has actually observed; that is, one cannot put into evidence the out-of-court statement of another to prove the truth of that statement.

   b. **Exceptions to hearsay rule.** There are exceptions to the hearsay rule. One of these is the "admissions exception"—anything that the defendant himself has said out of court can be introduced in court to prove the truth of the fact asserted in the out-of-court statement. Also, admissions by the agent of a party will often be received against the party. For example, if a truck driver hits A, then admits to A that he was going too fast, A may testify in court about the statement and such testimony will be used against the owner of the truck and the employer of the driver (*i.e.*, the principal).

4. **Mens Rea.**

   a. **Specific intent.** Conspiracy is generally held to be a specific intent crime; that is, the defendant must have the specific intent to commit the act that is a crime.

   b. **Is knowledge enough?** To be guilty of a conspiracy, one must have more than mere knowledge. There has to be an improper purpose or desire; *i.e.*, the defendant must in some sense promote the venture herself, make it her own, or have a stake in its outcome.

c. **Intent to kill--**

People v. Swain, 909 P.2d 994 (Cal. 1996).

Facts. Swain and Chapman (Ds) were on trial for a drive-by shooting in which a 15-year-old boy was killed. Swain denied being in the van from which the shots were fired. Chapman admitted to being in the van and firing shots, but claimed that he fired in self defense after hearing other shots fired. The jury was instructed that the target offense of the conspiracy was murder in the second degree. The jury found Chapman guilty of second degree murder and conspiracy and found Swain guilty of conspiracy. As to both Ds, the jury made a finding under the conspiracy count that the target offense of the conspiracy was murder in the second degree. Ds appeal.

Issue. Is intent to kill a required element of conspiracy to commit murder?

Held. Yes. Judgment reversed.

- ♦ Conspiracy is a "specific intent" crime, and a conviction must be supported by a showing of: (i) the intent to conspire, and (ii) the intent to commit the elements of the target offense.

- ♦ The target offense in this case was found to be murder in the second degree. Under California law, murder in the second degree may be based on one of three theories: (i) unpremeditated murder with express malice (intent to kill); (ii) implied malice murder; or (iii) second degree felony murder.

- ♦ The jury was instructed on the principles of implied malice second degree murder. However, implied malice does not require a finding of an intent to kill. In contrast to express malice murder, implied malice murder requires an intent to do some act that is dangerous to human life. The required mental state for conviction of conspiracy to commit murder is an intent to kill; thus a conviction cannot be based on a theory of implied malice.

d. **Provider of services--**

People v. Lauria, 59 Cal. Rptr. 628 (Cal. Ct. App. 1967).

Facts. Lauria (D) ran a telephone answering service. D knew that some of his clients were prostitutes, but he permitted them to use his telephone service anyway. After infiltration by a policewoman, D and three prostitutes were indicted for conspiracy to commit prostitution. The trial court set aside the indictment for lack of probable cause. The People appeal.

Issue. May a person be guilty of conspiracy for knowingly providing legitimate services that are used to commit misdemeanors when he has no stake in the venture?

Held. No. Judgment affirmed.

- Knowledge of another's criminal activity is not necessarily a conspiracy to further the activity. A supplier of goods or services has a variable duty to screen his customers. In *United States v. Falcone*, 311 U.S. 205 (1940), distributors of sugar, yeast, and cans were found not guilty of conspiracy to produce illegal liquor. However, in *Direct Sales Co. v. United States*, 319 U.S. 703 (1943), a drug wholesaler was convicted of conspiracy with the buyer, who was supplying addicts.

- Knowledge of an illegal use must be coupled with intent to further that use in order to justify the supplier's conspiracy conviction. Proof of intent may be established by direct evidence or by evidence of circumstances from which such intent may be inferred.

- If direct evidence of intent is lacking, as here, intent may be inferred when there is knowledge and: (i) the person has acquired a stake in the illegal venture; (ii) no legitimate use for the goods or services exists; or (iii) the volume of business with the buyer is grossly disproportionate to any legitimate demand, or sales for illegal use amount to a high proportion of the seller's total business.

- The nature of the crime is relevant because a person has a duty to take positive action to dissociate himself from activities helpful to felonies. Providing unusual amounts of drugs to a customer may imply an intent to participate in the wrongful use of such drugs. However, an inference of intent drawn from knowledge of criminal use does not apply to the less serious crimes classified as misdemeanors.

- In this case, D did not take any direct action to further, encourage, or direct the prostitute activities of his customers. He did not charge excessive fees for his services or have an unusual amount of business with prostitutes. Thus, there was insufficient proof of his participation in a criminal conspiracy.

---

5. **Actus Reus.** The actus reus of conspiracy is the entering into of the requisite agreement.

   a. **Nature of the agreement.** The agreement need not be an express or formal one but can be implied from the cooperative actions of the parties. Thus, for instance, one who observes unlawful acts taking place and cooperates in their commission may become a member of an agreement to carry out those acts, even if the participants never formally exchanged express commitments with each other.

b. **Connecting one to existing agreement.** Similarly, if the existence of a conspiracy is clearly shown, relatively slight evidence will be sufficient to connect a particular defendant with it.

c. **Overt act.** At common law, no act is required beyond the making of the agreement, *i.e.*, the crime is complete when the agreement is reached with the requisite intent. But while many jurisdictions still adhere to the common law rule, some modern statutes impose the additional requirement of an "overt act."

   1) The overt act, where required, must be one to effect the object of the conspiracy or that has a tendency to further the objective. Hence, conversations among the parties planning the crime are not "overt acts."

   2) At the same time, however, any single act in pursuit of the unlawful objective by ***any one*** of the members will suffice. At this point, all parties to the agreement become liable for conspiracy.

d. **Sufficiency of evidence--**

Commonwealth v. Azim, 459 A.2d 1244 (Pa. Super. Ct. 1983).

Facts. Azim (D) was the driver of a car in which James and Robinson were passengers. D stopped the car, and Robinson called out to the victim. When the victim did not respond, James and Robinson got out of the car, assaulted the victim, and took his wallet. D then drove James and Robinson from the scene. At trial, D was convicted as a co-defendant. D appeals.

Issue. Was there sufficient evidence to find a conspiracy?

Held. Yes. Judgment affirmed.

- The essence of a criminal conspiracy is a common understanding that a particular criminal objective be accomplished. Often a conspiracy can only be proven by circumstantial evidence. Although a conspiracy cannot be based on suspicion or conjecture, it may be established by the relationship, conduct, and acts of co-conspirators.

- In this case, D drove the car and was sitting next to Robinson when Robinson called the victim over to the car. D stayed in the car with the engine running, the lights on, and the doors open, while the victim was assaulted and robbed. D then drove the other two defendants from the scene of the crime.

- Some of the relevant circumstances in proving a conspiracy are: (i) association with the alleged conspirators, (ii) knowledge of the commission of the crime, (iii) presence at the scene, and, at times, (iv) participation in the object of the conspiracy.

- A rational factfinder could find beyond a reasonable doubt that D conspired with his co-defendants to commit assault and robbery. Once a conspiracy is proven, each member of the conspiracy is also guilty of the criminal acts of his co-conspirators.

---

e. **Accomplice or conspirator?--**

Commonwealth v. Cook, 411 N.E.2d 1326 (Mass. App. Ct. 1980).

Facts. The victim, a 17-year-old woman, was on her way to visit her boyfriend when she came upon Cook (D) and his brother, Maurice. They tried to engage her in conversation, but because she did not know them, the victim continued toward her boyfriend's house. After finding that her boyfriend was not home, she headed back and again saw D and Maurice. This time she sat with the two brothers and talked in an area that was used as a common meeting place for socializing. Because she was having difficulty remembering the brothers' names, D showed the victim his work identification card, and Maurice showed her his driver's license. After a while, Maurice suggested that the three of them walk to a nearby convenience store so that he could buy cigarettes. As they walked toward a path to the store, the victim fell. Maurice then jumped on her and forcibly raped her. Subsequently, Maurice was indicted for rape, and D was indicted for conspiracy to commit rape. D was convicted on the indictment. D appeals.

Issue. Can an accomplice be convicted for conspiracy if there was no agreement to pursue a particular criminal objective?

Held. No. Judgment reversed.

- A conviction for conspiracy requires proof of the existence of an agreement, and it must be shown that the defendant was aware of the objective of the conspiracy. Although the proof may be based on circumstantial evidence, it may not be based on conjecture or guesswork.

- In this case, the victim and the brothers met by chance. The brothers did not try to conceal from others that they were with the victim as they talked. They also did not try to conceal their identities from the victim. Their highly visible conduct is inconsistent with the clandestine nature of a conspiracy. Furthermore, all of the conversation took place in the victim's presence, making it doubtful that they could have formulated a plan to assault her. Moreover, the circumstances surrounding the rape do not suggest a predetermined plan. Although a tacit agreement may be sufficient to establish a conspiracy, here it is just as reasonable to conclude that D became implicated in the crime as an accomplice after it had begun, without any advance knowledge that it was going to happen.

- D cannot be convicted of conspiracy solely on evidence showing his complicity as an accomplice. Liability as an accomplice is not the same as liability as a co-conspirator. One can be an accomplice during the commission of a crime without having conspired to commit it. The essence of conspiracy is the agreement between the conspirators to work together for an unlawful purpose. This agreement manifests the requisite criminal intent for conspiracy. The establishment of such an agreement is absent from the formulation of accomplice liability. Although acts of aiding and abetting make each actor a principal in the substantive offense, they cannot, without more, make each actor a conspirator.

---

6. Conspiracy: Bilateral or Unilateral?

a. Bilateral theory--

People v. Foster, 457 N.E.2d 405 (Ill. 1983).

Facts. Foster (D) initiated a plan to commit robbery when he approached John Ragsdale in a bar. D stated his plan to rob an elderly man, Hedrick, whom he knew to have valuables in his home, and D asked Ragsdale's assistance. Ragsdale was not interested in following through with the crime but wanted to gather information about the plan in order to report D to the police. A few days after their initial meeting, D went to Ragsdale's home and asked him if he was "ready to go." Ragsdale stalled and then informed the police of the planned robbery. Three days later, D and Ragsdale went to Hedrick's residence, and D was arrested. D was convicted of conspiracy to commit robbery, but his conviction was reversed by the appellate court. The state appeals.

Issue. Can a conspiracy be proven if only one party is involved?

Held. No. Judgment reversed.

- The appellate court determined that the Illinois conspiracy statute requires actual agreement between at least two persons to support a conspiracy conviction. Reasoning that Ragsdale never intended to agree to D's plan, they reversed D's conviction.

- The state argues that under the statute it suffices if only one of the participants to the alleged conspiracy actually intends to commit the offense.

- Illinois's amended conspiracy statute states: "A person commits conspiracy when, with intent that an offense be committed, he agrees with another to the commission of that offense."

- The state contends that Illinois's conspiracy statute is similar to the Model Penal Code conspiracy provision, which clearly states in the commentary the drafters' intent to adopt a unilateral theory of conspiracy.

- If the drafters of the Illinois statute had intended to adopt the unilateral theory of conspiracy, they would have made this clear in their comments, which they did not. Furthermore, the Illinois solicitation statute covers every situation in which one could be convicted of conspiracy under the unilateral theory, and the penalties for solicitation and conspiracy are substantially similar.

---

7. **Scope of Conspiracy.** When a conspiracy involves many parties, the issue frequently arises as to whether there was one large conspiracy or several smaller ones. This is an important issue as it relates to both charging and trying the offense. The prosecution's task may be simplified by charging one large conspiracy so that all the parties involved are tried in one proceeding because it saves time and can result in expanded admissibility of evidence; however, this approach risks unfairness to defendants whose actual involvement was limited to a smaller, distinct conspiracy.

   a. **Patterns of conspiracies.**

      1) **Chain.** When a series of transactions is involved, each transaction may be treated as a "link" in one overall "chain." So long as the parties to each link transaction have a general interest in the success of the overall series of transactions, the scheme will be treated as a single large conspiracy. This is not the case if the various transactions are truly separate.

      2) **Wheel and spoke.** If one person (a hub of a wheel) enters into a number of different transactions with various other persons (the spokes) who are unconcerned with the other transactions entered into by the hub, the various transactions are deemed to be different conspiracies. The fact that each has one common co-conspirator is irrelevant if the various spokes share no common objective.

         a) **"Wheel" conspiracy--**

Kilgore v. State, 305 S.E.2d 82 (Ga. 1983).

Facts. Kilgore (D) was charged with the murder of Roger Norman. At trial, the state introduced evidence of a conspiracy to kill Norman and three previous attempts on Norman's life. David Oldaker testified that his cousin Benton described a man named Tom who wanted Norman killed. Oldaker and Benton went to Norman's home to kill him but were unsuccessful. Another witness testified that Norman was later shot near Trenton, Georgia, by someone driving a Rambler. D's ex-girlfriend, Constance Chambers, testified that on the day of that shooting, D and his cousin had borrowed her Rambler, which fit the description of the one involved in the shooting. D told her that he and his cousin had killed a man near Trenton, but she later heard him talking on the phone to Tom Carden and saying, "apparently we didn't get him." In a later phone conversation with Carden, D told him that he needed more money to get a faster car. Chambers then went with D to Carden's trailer, where D took $15,000 from the mailbox. Chambers and D met up with a friend of D, and D took a rifle from his car and put it into his friend's van. D and his friend left in the van, and Chambers drove home. Chambers further testified that, several days later, D told her that he and his friend had killed a man. D was convicted for the murder of Norman and was given a life sentence. D appeals.

Issue. When one person deals with others having no connection with each other and no community of interests, are all of them guilty of one conspiracy?

Held. No, but no reversible error. Judgment affirmed.

- D argues that the state proceeded on the theory that his guilt was based on a conspiracy. D also argues that the trial court erred in admitting Oldaker's hearsay testimony of Benton's description of the man who wanted Norman killed, which fit the description of Tom Carden. Oldaker's hearsay testimony of Benton's description of Tom was the only evidence linking Tom Carden to Oldaker's attempt on Norman's life. This testimony could only be admissible under the exception to the hearsay rule that provides that the out-of-court statements of one conspirator are admissible against all conspirators. Thus, this testimony was only admissible if Oldaker, Benton, and D were co-conspirators.

- Oldaker, Benton, and Carden were co-conspirators in their attempt to kill Norman. D, his friend, and Carden were co-conspirators in Norman's murder. However, D did not know of or communicate with Oldaker and Benton, and Oldaker and Benton did not know of or communicate with D.

- It is possible for different people to be parties to a conspiracy even though they do not know each other and even though they are not all aware of the details of the plans under the conspiracy. A single conspiracy may be inferred in what has been termed a "chain" conspiracy, in which there is successive communication or cooperation. The parties involved in a large, ongoing conspiracy of this kind (*e.g.*, the distribution of narcotics) should know that other members exist. The various "links" in such a conspiracy have a community of interest because the success of one member's part is dependent on the success of the whole enterprise. Thus, courts have treated these links as co-conspirators even if they do not communicate or have contact with each other.

- In contrast, there is a "wheel" conspiracy in which there is usually a "hub," or common source of the conspiracy, who deals individually with different persons, or "spokes," who do not know each other. These persons are less likely to have a community of interests or a reason to know of each other's existence because one's success is usually not dependent on the success of the others, but depends on his dealings with the "hub."

- ♦ Here, D was not a co-conspirator of Oldaker and Benton because there was no community of interests between Oldaker and Benton on the one hand and D on the other. Furthermore, Oldaker and Benton, as one "spoke," and D, as a replacement "spoke," had no knowledge of each other. Therefore, they could not have agreed to and become co-conspirators in Norman's murder. Although the trial court erred in admitting Oldaker's hearsay testimony, the error was harmless.

---

b. **Multiple unlawful purposes.** Numerous separate crimes may be contemplated by one overall agreement. Such an agreement constitutes a single conspiracy, even though there is more than one unlawful purpose.

1) **One agreement, one conspiracy--**

Braverman v. United States, 317 U.S. 49 (1942).

Facts. Braverman (D) and others collaborated in the illicit manufacture, transportation, and distribution of distilled spirits in violation of several internal revenue laws. D was convicted on several counts, each charging a conspiracy to violate a different law.

Issue. May co-conspirators whose conspiracy violates more than one law be convicted of conspiracy as to each law violated?

Held. No. Judgment reversed.

- ♦ Where there is only one conspiracy agreement, but the object of such a conspiracy violates several statutes or different provisions of a single statute, the defendants can be convicted only for the single conspiracy and not for multiple conspiracies for each illegal object. The one agreement cannot be taken to be several agreements.

---

c. **Unknown conspirators.** It is not necessary that the parties to a conspiracy know the identity of each member, or even that they be aware of the number of persons involved. A co-conspirator is deemed to have conspired with all those he must have known were involved in the transaction, whether he had specific information about them or not.

8. **Defenses.**

a. **Wharton's Rule.** Some crimes require a preliminary agreement among the participants as an inherent prerequisite to the commission of the crime. These are offenses that can only be committed by the ***concerted action*** of two or more persons. These offenses are subject to Wharton's Rule, which imposes special limitations upon conspiracy law.

1) **Basic prohibition.** Wharton's Rule holds that where persons are charged with conspiracy to commit an offense, which by its definition requires a preliminary agreement between the parties, there can be no conviction for conspiracy. The classic cases are adultery, incest, bigamy, and dueling. Since an agreement or concerted action is an essential element of each of these offenses, the two participants cannot be prosecuted for conspiracy to commit the offense.

2) **Exceptions.**

a) **"Third-party exception"—more than essential participants.** When the number of conspirators exceeds the essential participants in the contemplated crime (*e.g.*, D conspires with A and B for the commission of adultery by the latter two), a number of courts do not apply Wharton's Rule. All of the parties to the agreement may be convicted of conspiracy, because they have formed a group larger than is necessary for the commission of the crime.

b) **Objective of agreement not achieved.** Some courts will apply Wharton's Rule only where the parties have accomplished their objective, so that the Rule only bars conviction for both conspiracy and the completed crime. Others, however, criticize this limitation, and many decisions have not recognized it.

3) **Rule as a presumption.** The United States Supreme Court in *Iannelli, infra*, has held that Wharton's Rule is merely a presumption of legislative intent. Thus, if the Rule would bar conviction in a given case, but there is also evidence of a legislative intent to impose liability, the legislative intent controls and criminal sanctions may be imposed.

4) **Leading case--**

Iannelli v. United States, 420 U.S. 770 (1975).

Facts. Iannelli and seven others (Ds) were convicted of both conspiring to violate and violating a federal gambling statute. The statute made it a crime for five or more people to conduct (own, supervise, etc.) a gambling business prohibited by state law. After the convictions, Ds appealed to the circuit court, which affirmed on the ground that the convictions came within the "third-party exception" to Wharton's Rule (discussed above). The Supreme Court granted certiorari.

Issue. Is Wharton's Rule a presumption (to be applied absent contrary legislative intent) rather than a principle based on the Double Jeopardy Clause?

Held. Yes. Judgment affirmed.

- Generally, conspiracy and the substantive offenses are separate crimes. Congressional statutes, absent indications to the contrary, recognize the separate offenses doctrine. Wharton's Rule, then, is an exception to this general rule.

- The Rule does not rest upon principles of double jeopardy; rather, it is a judicial presumption to be applied in the absence of contrary legislative intent.

- Here, the statute involved is significantly different from the offenses to which the Rule has traditionally been applied. In the cases where the Rule has historically been applied, the harm has been between the parties involved. Here, large-scale gambling activities designed to elicit the participation of additional persons are involved. These activities are of much broader scope than the Rule has traditionally covered.

- Furthermore, the Rule applies only to offenses that by their nature require concerted activity (adultery, bigamy, incest, etc.). The offense involved here does not require concerted activity.

- Here, there is no indication that Congress intended to foreclose the possibility of prosecuting offenders for both conspiracy and the substantive offense. Therefore, the exception to the general rule afforded by Wharton's Rule is not applicable.

---

b. **Two guilty parties required--**

Gebardi v. United States, 287 U.S. 112 (1932).

Facts. Gebardi (D) and the woman he transported across state lines to have sexual relations with were charged with a conspiracy to violate the Mann Act (which prohibited interstate transportation of women for immoral purposes). Gebardi made all of the arrangements; the woman voluntarily consented to go. Ds were convicted of conspiracy to violate the Mann Act. The Supreme Court granted certiorari.

Issue. If one person agrees with another to commit a crime, can one person be guilty of a conspiracy even if the other is not?

Held. No. Judgment reversed.

- Congress intended the Mann Act to exempt the woman of the substantive crime. Therefore, the woman may not be convicted of conspiracy to violate the Act. Since she is not guilty, the man cannot be either, since it takes two persons for a conspiracy (there must be an "agreement").

Comment. The Model Penal Code would convict the man in *Gebardi*, but most courts follow the *Gebardi* rule.

---

c. **Withdrawal as defense--**

People v. Sconce, 279 Cal. Rptr. 59 (Cal. Ct. App. 1991).

Facts. Sconce (D) offered Garcia $10,000 to kill Estephan. Garcia agreed to commit the murder or find someone to do it. Garcia then contacted Dutton and offered him $5,000 to kill Estephan. Garcia and Dutton went to Estephan's house and made a plan to plant a bomb under his car. Approximately three weeks after their initial conversation, D contacted Garcia and "called it off." The People filed an information charging D with conspiracy to commit murder. The trial court set the information aside. The People appeal.

Issue. Is withdrawal a valid defense to conspiracy once an overt act has occurred?

Held. No. The order seting the information aside is reversed.

- The People argue that although D's withdrawal might insulate him from liability for future conspiratorial acts, it does not constitute a defense to liability for the conspiracy itself.

- Once a defendant's participation in a conspiracy is shown, it is presumed to continue unless he is able to prove that he effectively withdrew from the conspiracy.

- Under California law, withdrawal is a complete defense to conspiracy, but only if it is accomplished before the commission of an overt act. Once an overt act has been committed in furtherance of the conspiracy, the crime of conspiracy has been completed.

- Withdrawal precludes liability from subsequent acts committed by members of the conspiracy but does not relate back to the criminal formation of the conspiracy. Here, even if D withdrew from the conspiracy, he was still criminally liable for the conspiracy itself because overt acts had been committed in furtherance of the conspiracy.

XI. LIABILITY FOR THE CONDUCT OF ANOTHER

A. ACCOMPLICE LIABILITY

1. General Principles.

a. **Common law.** The common law distinguished four types of parties to a felony: (i) ***principals in the first degree*** (persons who actually engage in the act or omission that constitutes the criminal offense); (ii) ***principals in the second degree*** (persons who aid, command, or encourage the principal and are present, either actively or constructively, at the crime); (iii) ***accessories before the fact*** (persons who aid, abet, or encourage the principal but are not present at the crime); and (iv) ***accessories after the fact*** (persons who, with knowledge of the other's guilt, assist the principal after the crime). [*See* State v. Ward, 396 A.2d 1041 (Md. 1978)]

1) **Significance of common law distinctions.** At common law, the distinctions between the parties had a great deal of procedural significance. For example, an accessory could not be convicted unless the principal had already been convicted, although both could be convicted in a joint trial if the jury determined the principal's guilt first. Most modern jurisdictions have abandoned this requirement, and an accessory can be convicted even if the principal has evaded apprehension or has been tried and acquitted.

b. **Modern statutes.** Most jurisdictions have abolished the distinctions between principals in the first degree, principals in the second degree, and accessories before the fact (accessories after the fact are still treated separately). Under the modern approach, all "parties to the crime" can be found guilty of the criminal offense.

1) **Principal.** A principal is one who, with the requisite mental, ***actually engages in the act or omission*** that causes the criminal result. Also, anyone who acts through an innocent, irresponsible, or unwilling agent is classified as a principal. For example, A gives a poisonous drink to B to give to C. B does so. C drinks it and dies. If B did not know that the drink was poisonous, or if B was mentally ill or under duress, A, not B, is the principal. Note that the principal need not be present when the harm results.

2) **Accomplice.** An accomplice is one who, with the intent that the crime be committed, aids, counsels, or encourages the principal before or during the commission of the crime.

3) **Accessory after the fact.** An accessory after the fact is one who receives, relieves, comforts, or assists another, knowing that he has committed a felony, in order to ***help the felon escape arrest, trial, or conviction***. The crime committed by the principal must be a felony and it must be completed at the time the aid is rendered. Today, the crime is usually called "harboring a fugitive," "aiding escape," or "obstructing justice."

   a) **Penalty.** Typically, the punishment for this crime bears no relationship to the principal offense; five years is the most common maximum sentence. Exemptions are usually provided for close relatives of the principal offender (the common law exempted only the spouse).

2. **Elements of Accomplice Liability--**

State v. Hoselton, 371 S.E.2d 366 (W. Va. 1988).

Facts. Eighteen-year-old Kevin Hoselton (D) went with friends to a docked barge. His friends stole tools, grease guns, grease, and a battery charger from the storage unit of the barge. In both a voluntary statement given before trial and at trial, D stated that he was standing at one end of the barge with an obstructed view of the storage unit and was unaware of his friends' intent to steal the items until he heard the door of the storage unit open. When he walked to the unit, he saw his friends with the goods. Then D went to the car of one of his friends, his friends joined him with the goods, and D was driven home. In his statement and during trial, D stated that he had no prior knowledge that his friends intended to steal anything from the barge. When he saw his friends removing goods from the storage unit, he left the barge and returned to the car. He did not receive any of the stolen property. D also testified that he and his friends often trespassed on the barge for fishing. D was convicted of entering without breaking a vessel, with intent to commit larceny. D appeals.

Issue. To be convicted of aiding and abetting, must a defendant give assistance or encouragement in the crime with the intent to promote or facilitate the commission of the crime?

Held. Yes. Judgment reversed.

- The state contends that there was sufficient evidence to establish that D was a lookout. A lookout is one who, by prearrangement, keeps watch to avoid detection or to provide warning during the perpetration of a crime. Lookouts are aiders and abettors, principals in the second degree.

- To convict a defendant as an aider and abettor, it must be demonstrated that the defendant somehow associated himself with the venture and participated in it so that his actions would help the venture to succeed. It must be shown that the defendant shared the criminal intent of the principal in the first degree.

- ♦ Here, the only evidence suggesting that D was a lookout was his response to the investigating officer's questioning when D gave his voluntary statement. When the officer asked D if he was a lookout, D answered, "You could say that. I just didn't want to go down in there." This statement, standing alone, does not establish that D was an aider and abettor.

---

3. **Mens Rea.** Criminal liability for the acts of others is predicated on the individual's criminal intent. When the defendant did not actually perform the crime, but only assisted in some way, determination of the necessary mens rea is often difficult.

   a. **Intent: "purpose" or "knowledge"?** To be convicted as an accomplice under the prevailing common law rule, a person must have given aid, counsel, or encouragement with the intent to aid or encourage the principal in the commission of the crime charged. In the absence of a statute, most courts would hold that mere knowledge that a crime would result from the aid provided is insufficient for accomplice liability, at least where the aid involves the sale of ordinary goods at ordinary prices; thus, procuring an illegal item or selling at a higher price because of the buyer's purpose may constitute a sufficient "stake in the venture" for a court to find intent to aid. Other courts determine whether a person is guilty as an accomplice, not on whether he had a stake in the venture, but merely on whether he aided and assisted the perpetrators. Thus, one who profits by selling goods or services to another, knowing that this is enabling the other to carry out a crime, could be found guilty of aiding the criminal. Consider how these different views would affect the defendant in *People v. Lauria*, *supra*, if he had been prosecuted as an accomplice, rather than as a co-conspirator, of the prostitutes who used his answering service.

   b. **When is "intent" not required?**

      1) **Culpability for unintended result--**

Riley v. State, 60 P.3d 204 (Alaska Ct. App. 2002).

Facts. Riley (D) and another man opened fire on a crowd of unsuspecting young people, seriously wounding two of them. The physical evidence showed that the wounds were inflicted by one of the two guns used by the men, but the ballistics analysis could not prove which gun fired the wounding shots. At trial, the jurors were instructed that they should decide whether D acted as a principal or, if they could not decide beyond a reasonable doubt which man fired the shots, they should decide whether D acted as an accomplice in the wounding of the victims. D was found guilty as an accomplice in the wounding of both victims. D appeals.

Issue. When a person is charged as an accomplice in a crime that requires proof of a particular result, must the government prove that the person acted intentionally with respect to that particular result?

Held. No. Judgment affirmed.

- In *Echols v. State*, 818 P.2d 691 (Alaska Ct. App. 1991), a wife was charged as an accomplice to first degree assault. She had summoned her husband to discipline their child and stood by and watched as he inflicted serious physical injury on the child. The court held that the wife could be held accountable as an accomplice to the assault only if the state proved that she acted intentionally with respect to the prohibited result (*i.e.*, that her conscious objective was to have the child suffer serious physical injury).

- The holding in *Echols* has counterintuitive consequences when the underlying offense is defined in terms of an ***unintended result***, because accomplice liability would require proof that the defendant acted ***intentionally*** with respect to the particular result. Thus, the state would have to prove a higher culpable mental state for the accomplice than for the principal. We now overrule our decision in *Echols*.

- Under our state's complicity statute, accomplice liability requires "intent to promote or facilitate the commission of the offense." The standard interpretation of this phrase is that it requires proof of the accomplice's intent to promote or facilitate another's conduct that constitutes the actus reus of the offense. As to the results of that conduct, the government must prove that the accomplice had the same culpable mental state that is required for the underlying crime.

- Whether D acted as a principal or an accomplice, the applicable mental state was recklessness as to the possibility that the conduct would cause serious injury. Because this culpable mental state was established, we affirm D's convictions.

---

2) Foreseeable consequence rule--

State v. Linscott, 520 A.2d 1067 (Me. 1987).

Facts. Linscott (D) participated in a planned robbery of a known drug dealer. He drove to the victim's house with another party, Fuller, with the intent to rob the victim. D was armed with a knife, and Fuller was armed with a shotgun. After arriving at the victim's house, D broke the living room window of the house. Fuller fired a shot through the broken window, hitting the victim in the chest and killing him. The court found that D had the intent to commit the crime of robbery, that Fuller intentionally or at least knowingly caused the death of the victim, and that this murder was a reasonably foreseeable consequence of D's participation in the robbery. The court also found that D had no intent to kill the victim and probably would not have participated in the robbery had he believed that the victim would be killed. D was convicted of murder and robbery. D appeals.

Issue. Does the "foreseeable consequence" rule of accomplice liability violate a defendant's constitutional right to due process?

Held. No. Judgment affirmed.

- D contends that he lacked the requisite intent to be convicted of intentional or knowing murder.
- The history of our state's accomplice liability statute shows that the legislature intended to impose liability upon accomplices for those crimes that were the reasonably foreseeable consequence of their criminal enterprise, notwithstanding an absence on their part of the same culpability required for conviction as a principal to the crime.
- Accomplice liability for the "primary crime" (here, robbery) is established by proof that the accomplice intended to promote or facilitate that crime. Accomplice liability for the "secondary crime" (here, murder) is established by showing that: (i) the accomplice intended to promote the primary crime, and (ii) the commission of the secondary crime was a foreseeable consequence of the accomplice's participation in the primary crime.
- Allowing a murder conviction under a theory of accomplice liability based on an objective standard, despite the absence of evidence that the defendant possessed the culpable subjective mental state that constitutes an element of the crime of murder, is not a departure from our prior law and is not in violation of D's right to due process.

---

4. **Actus Reus.** In deciding whether particular conduct is such as would justify criminal liability, the materiality of aid or encouragement is a major factor. The "but for" test used to determine causation need not be satisfied for a determination of accessorial liability, as long as the necessary mens rea is present. The threshold of materiality of the act is not always clear, however.

    a. **Active participation?--**

State v. Vaillancourt, 453 A.2d 1327 (N.H. 1982).

Facts. Vaillancourt (D) and another man, Burhoe, stood together on the front porch of a house, ringing the doorbell for approximately 10 minutes. The two young men then walked to the side of the house, and D watched as Burhoe allegedly attempted to break into a basement window. A witness called the police, and the two men were apprehended as they were fleeing the scene. D was convicted for accomplice liability in connection with an attempted burglary. D appeals.

Issue. Are the acts of accompaniment and observation sufficient to constitute "aid"?

Held. No. Judgment reversed.

- The crime of accomplice liability requires the actor to have solicited, aided, agreed to aid, or attempted to aid the principal in planning or committing the offense. Knowledge and mere presence at the scene do not support a conviction for accomplice liability; there must be some active participation to satisfy the actus reus requirement. The trial court erred in ruling that the indictment was sufficient on its face, because D's acts of accompanying and observing Burhoe were not sufficient to constitute "aid."

Dissent. The indictment in this case alleged more than "mere presence." The indictment alleged the requisite mens rea, and it also alleged accompaniment, which connotes some further connection between the accomplice and the principal. Accompaniment with the purpose of aiding implies the furnishing of moral support and encouragement in the performance of a crime.

---

b. Encouraging commission of an illegal act--

Wilcox v. Jeffery, 1 All E.R. 464 (1951).

Facts. Without an immigration officer's grant of leave to land, aliens were forbidden to take employment, paid or unpaid, while in the United Kingdom. Hawkins, a United States saxophone player, was invited to the United Kingdom by two men who were connected with a jazz club. They applied for permission for Hawkins to land, but permission was refused. Wilcox (D), who owned a jazz music magazine, greeted Hawkins upon his arrival, attended a jazz concert given by Hawkins, and wrote and published an article praising the illegal concert. D was convicted of aiding and abetting Hawkins in violating the alien order. D appeals.

Issue. May a person be guilty of aiding and abetting a criminal act simply by being a paid spectator at the event and by publishing an article about it?

Held. Yes. Judgment affirmed.

- If D's presence had been accidental, he would probably not be guilty. But D took part in the illegal act by encouraging it, and he took advantage of it by writing about it in his magazine. D knew that the act was illegal, yet affirmatively encouraged its commission.

---

c. **Accomplice testimony--**

State v. Helmenstein, 163 N.W.2d 85 (N.D. 1968).

Facts. Helmenstein (D) and five other young people drank some beer at a park and then drove around in D's car. One of them suggested that they break into a store in a town about six miles away. They drove to the store, and three of them, including D, broke in and got beer, cigarettes, candy, and bananas. While driving from the store, the young people all agreed on a story that they would tell the police if they were questioned. They divided the goods and separated. At trial, five of them testified against D. The only other witness was the store owner, but he could only testify that on the morning after the burglary, he found that the store had been burglarized and about $130 worth of merchandise had been taken. His testimony merely established that a crime had been committed but did not connect D with the crime. D was found guilty of burglary and appeals.

Issue. Is the uncorroborated testimony of accomplices connecting the defendant to a crime sufficient evidence to maintain a conviction?

Held. No. Judgment reversed.

- The statute provides that a conviction may not be had upon the testimony of an accomplice unless his testimony is corroborated by such other evidence that tends to connect the defendant with the commission of the offense, and the corroboration is not sufficient if it merely shows the commission of the offense or the circumstances.

- In this case, two of the young people testified that they had secret objections to the burglary, which they did not express to the others. Instead of objecting, one of the two said that she wanted bananas when the idea of the burglary was brought up. The other testified that he fell asleep during the burglary, but not until the three who committed the burglary had left the car and headed for the store. Also, he testified that everyone in the group together made up the story to mislead the police. Furthermore, another person in the group testified that everyone in the group agreed to the burglary.

- Because the burglary was the result of a plan that each of the young people encouraged, they are all accomplices. Since there is no other evidence connecting D with the commission of the crime, the evidence against him is insufficient.

---

d. **Causation and complicity.** In *State ex rel. Martin v. Tally*, 15 So. 722 (Ala. 1894), the court found that the judge was an accomplice in the killing of the deceased because he deprived the deceased of a chance of life. The deceased's relatives had sent him a telegram warning him that he was being sought after for the seduction of the judge's sister-in-law. The judge, however, advised the telegraph operator not to deliver the warning telegram. Ultimately, the assailants caught up with the deceased and killed him. The court concluded that one can be held criminally responsible if he renders it easier for the principal actor to accomplish the intended act, even though it would have been attained without such help.

e. **Underlying crime not committed--**

People v. Genoa, 470 N.W.2d 447 (Mich. Ct. App. 1991).

Facts. An undercover police agent met with Genoa (D) and proposed that if D gave the agent $10,000 toward the purchase of a kilogram of cocaine, the agent would then sell the cocaine and repay D the $10,000, along with $3,500 in profits and a client list. D accepted the proposal, returned with the money, and was later arrested and charged with attempted possession with intent to deliver cocaine. The lower court dismissed the charge, and the prosecution appeals.

Issue. Can a defendant be convicted as an accessory if the underlying crime was not committed?

Held. No. Order dismissing the charge is affirmed.

- D did not attempt to possess the cocaine himself; his part was to help finance the proposed venture. Thus, D could have been prosecuted only under the theory that he attempted to aid and abet the crime of possession with intent to deliver cocaine.

- Although our state does not distinguish between principals and accessories for purposes of culpability, the following elements must be established to show that one aided and abetted the commission of a crime: (i) the underlying crime was committed by either the defendant or some other person; (ii) the defendant performed acts or gave encouragement that aided and assisted the commission of the crime; and (iii) the defendant intended the commission of the crime or had knowledge that the principal intended its commission at the time the defendant gave aid or encouragement. Here, the first element is missing, because the underlying crime was never committed. Therefore, it was legally impossible for D to have committed any offense.

5. Establishing Principal Liability--

Bailey v. Commonwealth, 329 S.E.2d 37, (Va. 1985).

Facts. Bailey (D) and Murdock began communicating over their citizens' band radios one evening. They had communicated in this manner in the past and cursed and threatened each other. D knew that Murdock was legally blind, that he owned a handgun, and that he was easily agitated. D also knew that on the night in question Murdock was intoxicated. D demanded that Murdoch arm himself with his handgun and wait on his front porch for D to come over to injure or kill him. D then made two anonymous calls to the local police to report a man on his porch waving a gun around. When three police arrived at Murdock's house, one of the officers asked him to leave his gun and opened fire. The officers returned fire and struck Murdock. As he lie dying, Murdock told the officers several times that he did not know that they were police. At trial, the jury was instructed that it should convict D if it found that his negligence or reckless conduct was so gross and culpable that it indicated a callous disregard for human life and that his actions were the proximate cause or a concurring cause of Murdock's death. D was convicted of involuntary manslaughter. D appeals.

Issue. Was D a principal in the first degree?

Held. Yes. Judgment affirmed.

- ♦ D argues that his conviction can only be sustained if he was a principal in the first degree, principal in the second degree, or an accessory before the fact. The attorney general maintains that D was a principal in the first degree.

- ♦ D argues that he could not be a principal in the first degree because he was not an immediate perpetrator of the crime.

- ♦ D contends that the officers who returned Murdock's fire were the immediate perpetrators of his killing. D points out that he was at home, two miles away from the confrontation. However, this state has adopted the rule that one who effects a criminal act through an innocent or unwitting agent is a principal in the first degree. It is irrelevant that D and the police did not share a common scheme or goal. What is relevant is that D used the police to accomplish his goal of causing Murdock harm.

- ♦ D also argues that Murdock's death was not the natural and probable result of his conduct because Murdock's act of opening fire on the police or the officers' return fire constituted an independent, intervening cause. However, an intervening act that is reasonably foreseeable cannot be relied upon as breaking the chain of causal connection between the original act and the subsequent injury. The confrontation between the police and Murdock was a reasonably foreseeable result of D's conduct.

6. Relationship of the Liability of the Accomplice to the Principal.

a. If principal is acquitted--

United States v. Lopez, 662 F. Supp. 1083 (N.D. Cal. 1987).

Facts. McIntosh (D) landed a helicopter on the grounds of a federal prison to help his girlfriend, Lopez (D), escape. They were apprehended 10 days later. Lopez contended that her life was unlawfully threatened by prison authorities. She and McIntosh planned to raise a necessity/duress defense based on the threats to her life. McIntosh and Lopez each filed a written offer of proof in camera to establish the prima facie case required for an instruction on the defense of necessity/duress. It was agreed that if Lopez made a prima facie showing of each element of the necessity/duress defense, she would be entitled to an instruction on that defense. McIntosh requested that the jury be instructed that if they found Lopez not guilty of escape because she acted under necessity/duress, they also had to find McIntosh not guilty of aiding and abetting her escape.

Issue. If a principal is found not guilty based on a necessity defense, must a defendant who aided and abetted the principal also be found not guilty?

Held. Yes. Jury instruction allowed.

- Although a defendant can be convicted of aiding and abetting even if the principal is not identified or convicted, he may not be held liable if there is no proof that the principal committed a crime.
- Lopez's necessity/duress defense must be classified as either a justification or an excuse. A defense is classified as a justification defense if the act committed was not wrongful. A defense is classified as an excuse if the act was wrongful but the actor will not be held accountable. A third party may assist a principal in a justified act and will not be held liable. On the other hand, excuses are personal to the actor.
- The defense of duress is generally raised if a person unlawfully commands another to do an unlawful act using the threat of death or serious bodily harm. The defense of necessity is raised if the actor chooses to violate the literal terms of the law in order to avoid a greater harm. The defense of necessity is categorized as a justification.
- Lopez's defense resembles necessity because she does not claim that threats overwhelmed her will, rendering her unable to make the correct choice; she claims that she made the correct choice to avoid a greater harm. Thus, if the jury finds her not guilty of escape because of necessity, her criminal act will be justified, and she will not have committed a crime. Since McIntosh should not be held liable if no crime was committed by Lopez, McIntosh is entitled to his requested jury instruction.

---

b. **If principal is convicted--**

People v. McCoy, 24 P3d 1210 (Cal. 2001).

Facts. McCoy and Lakey (D) were tried together and convicted of first degree murder arising out of a drive-by shooting. McCoy shot the victim but claimed self-defense. The jury rejected the defense, but the appellate court reversed McCoy's conviction on the ground that the trial judge had misinstructed the jury on the theory of imperfect (unreasonable) self-defense, and if the jury had accepted the imperfect self-defense claim, McCoy would have been guilty of manslaughter. The appellate court also reversed Lakey's conviction on the ground that, "under California law, a defendant who is tried as an aider and abettor cannot be convicted of an offense greater than that of which the actual perpetrator is convicted, where the aider and the perpetrator are tried in the same trial upon the same evidence." McCoy provided evidence at trial that he acted in unreasonable self-defense. Thus, it is possible that on retrial McCoy will be found guilty of manslaughter instead of murder. The People appeal the reversal of D's murder conviction.

Issue. Can an aider and abettor be guilty of a greater homicide-related offense than that which the perpetrator committed?

Held. Yes. Judgment reversed.

- The mental state required of an aider or abettor is different from the mental state necessary for the conviction as the actual perpetrator. However, this does not mean that the mental state of the aider and abettor is less culpable than that of the actual perpetrator; the mental state of the aider and abettor must be at least that of the perpetrator.

- Once it is established that the principal caused an actus reus, the liability of each of the secondary parties should be assessed according to his own mens rea. Although joint participants in a crime are tied to a single and common actus reus, the individual levels of guilt of the joint participants are not tied to each other.

- When a person, with the mental state necessary for an aider and abettor, helps or induces another to kill, that person's guilt is determined by the combined acts of all of the participants as well as that person's own mens rea. If that person's mens rea is more culpable than another's, that person's guilt may be greater even if the other is the actual perpetrator.

7. **Limits to Accomplice Liability.**

a. Member of class protected by statute--

In re Meagan R., 49 Cal. Rptr. 2d 325 (Cal. Ct. App. 1996).

Facts. Fourteen-year-old Meagan R. (D) assisted Oscar Rodriguez with breaking into the home of Rodriguez's ex-girlfriend so that D and Rodriguez could have sexual intercourse in the home. The juvenile court made true findings that D committed burglary based on a finding that she entered the home with the intent to aid and abet her own statutory rape. D appeals.

Issue. Can a minor who is the protected victim of statutory rape be prosecuted for her own statutory rape as an aider and abettor?

Held. No. Judgment reversed.

- If a crime necessarily involves the joint action of two or more persons, and the statute excludes one party from punishment, that party cannot be charged with criminal conduct on either a conspiracy or an aiding and abetting theory. Furthermore, when the legislature has imposed criminal penalties to protect a specific class of individuals, it could not have meant that a member of that class should be punished either as a co-conspirator or an aider and abettor.
- In this case, D was the protected victim of statutory rape under a provision that was designed to criminalize the exploitation of children, rather than to penalize the children themselves. Thus, D cannot be prosecuted for her own statutory rape, regardless of whether her culpability would be predicated on being a co-conspirator, an aider and abettor, or an accomplice.

---

b. Withdrawal after attempt--

People v. Brown, 414 N.E.2d 475 (Ill. App. Ct. 1980).

Facts. Brown (D), Schultz, and Babcock were driving around in Schultz's truck when Babcock suggested that they steal a car and wreck it. The three young men went to Hillside Motors, where the theft was to occur. Babcock told the other two to go to the back of the building and kick the door in and then he would enter the building and take keys and money while D and Schultz stood lookout. D and Schultz then went to the back of the building and kicked the door in, but they did not enter the building. D later told the assistant state's attorney that he got scared and decided to end his participation in the crime. He and Schultz told Babcock that they were leaving and taking the truck with them. Babcock reluctantly got into the truck with them. As they were leaving the parking lot of a service station next to Hillside Motors, they were stopped by the police. At trial, D was found guilty of attempt burglary. D appeals.

Issue. Is the withdrawal provision of Illinois's accountability statute applicable to an attempt charge against an aider and abettor if the attempt occurred before the withdrawal?

Held. No. Judgment affirmed.

- D argues that kicking the door in was mere preparation, rather than a substantial step toward the commission of the burglary. However, once the door was opened, the only step left was entry into the building. Thus, the act of kicking the door in was a substantial step.

- D also argues that he was not the principal and that he effectively withdrew from the criminal enterprise and prevented its completion. The withdrawal provision of the accountability statute provides that accountability is removed if, before the commission of the offense, the person terminates his efforts to promote it and makes a proper effort to prevent the commission of the offense. The offense referred to in the withdrawal provision is the offense in which the defendant aided or abetted.

- Here, burglary and attempt burglary are the possible offenses. D's withdrawal was effective as to the burglary because it occurred before the commission of a burglary. However, his withdrawal was ineffective as to the attempt burglary because his withdrawal did not occur before the commission of the attempt burglary.

B. VICARIOUS LIABILITY

Generally, criminal liability must be based on the defendant's own acts (or, in some cases, her failure to act). The major exception to this rule concerns those limited situations in which vicarious liability may be imposed.

1. **Definition—Liability for Acts of Others.** "Vicarious liability" is liability for the crimes committed by another person, imposed simply because of the relationship between the parties. In such situations, it is unnecessary to show that the defendant acted in any way or participated in the offense; it need only be established that the crime was committed by another and that the defendant stood in the required relationship to that person.

2. **When Vicarious Liability Is Imposed—Legislative Intent.** In practice, vicarious liability is ordinarily limited to employer-employee situations; *i.e.*, an employer is made vicariously liable for the crimes of her employees. However, in all cases, whether a statute creating a crime imposes vicarious liability depends upon the legislative intent; as a general rule, courts will assume that vicarious liability was not intended unless some indication to the contrary appears.

3. **Nature of Vicarious Liability.** As indicated above, where vicarious liability is imposed, the defendant is held accountable for the crimes committed by others whether she participated in them or not.

   a. **Crimes committed in disregard of instructions.** However, courts have split as to whether vicarious liability can be imposed where the employee (or other person for whose crimes the defendant would be vicariously liable) has committed the offense in disregard of the defendant's previous instructions.

4. **Policy Considerations.** Whether vicarious liability should be imposed as a matter of policy has been vigorously disputed.

   a. **Arguments favoring vicarious liability.** Those who support vicarious liability argue that it is essential to the effective enforcement of a number of important regulatory schemes, such as pure food regulations, prohibitions against child labor, etc.

   b. **Arguments against vicarious liability.** Nonetheless, it has also been stressed that vicarious liability is inconsistent with a basic principle of American criminal law that people should be held criminally liable only where they have demonstrated by their own actions that they are morally blameworthy.

5. **Criminal Liability for Acts of Employees--**

Commonwealth v. Koczwara, 155 A.2d 825 (Pa. 1959).

Facts. Koczwara (D) was the licensee and operator of a tavern. D's employees sold liquor to minors out of D's presence and without his personal knowledge. The Liquor Code prohibited such sales, and D was convicted of the offense. D was sentenced to three months in jail and fined $500. D appeals.

Issue. May a business owner be criminally liable for illegal sales made by his employees without his personal knowledge?

Held. Yes. Judgment affirmed, as modified.

- At common law, the respondeat superior doctrine would not apply in a criminal case because criminal liability was personal and individual. However, regulatory provisions in modern times rely on the criminal law for enforcement.

- Acceptance of a liquor license carries with it a high responsibility, including acceptance of vicarious liability for criminal violations by employees. The Liquor Code does not include a requirement of mens rea; thus, D's intent is irrelevant.

- Due process forbids imprisonment when liability is imposed vicariously. D's sentence must be modified to eliminate the imprisonment portion.

Dissent. If one may not be imprisoned for another's acts, it is equally wrong to convict him. A criminal conviction may do as much harm as a jail sentence.

C. CORPORATE LIABILITY

1. **Introduction.** Business crimes include traditional crimes committed in the course of doing legitimate business as well as violations of criminal regulatory statutes. The latter types of business crime, including antitrust violations, environmental protection violations, etc., present policy problems because they deviate in substantial ways from traditional criminal activity and therefore require a different kind of justification. In addition, when the crime is committed by a corporation, the liability of individual agents versus that of the entity is a major issue.

2. **Use of Criminal Law.**

   a. **Policy considerations.** When the criminal law is used to regulate the economic conduct of business (antitrust, price controls) or to promote public welfare objectives (environmental protection, consumer safety), the result is to undermine the restraints imposed on the use of criminal law generally.

      1) **Specificity.** A basic limitation on criminal statutes is that they must clearly describe the proscribed conduct. Many statutes have been declared void for vagueness. Yet the antitrust laws especially are notorious for not specifically defining what conduct is illegal.

      2) **Personal guilt.** Criminal justice requires that the person to be punished be personally guilty of the illegal act. Yet criminal sanctions on corporations fall on stockholders rather than on those who commit the crimes.

      3) **Deserved punishment.** Intent is a fundamental principle of criminal law because the stigma of criminal sanction should be reserved for those who intended the harm for which they are punished. Yet corporate punishment is far removed from those who intend the harm.

   b. **Deterrence.** Some commentators feel that criminal sanctions may make business too timid, stifling innovation. They contend that criminal sanctions provide excessive deterrence. Others feel that criminal sanctions would have an ideal deterrent effect. However, criminal penalties have not been effective in the area of business regulation.

1) One explanation is that business regulatory violations are not commonly regarded as morally reprehensible. The spirit of the free enterprise system denies moral culpability, thereby rendering criminal sanctions unjust.

2) Generally, the cases are complex. It is difficult to prove unlawful intent, and it is difficult to carry the burden of proof necessary to gain a criminal conviction.

3) Often the law is unclear as to what constitutes unlawful conduct.

4) Law enforcement is in the hands of members of a social class who are likely to sympathize with those in business.

3. **Effect on Individual Liability.** The imposition of corporate liability does ***not*** affect the criminal responsibility of the actual perpetrator. Thus, both the corporation and the guilty employee may be convicted of the offense.

4. **Corporation Liable for Specific Intent Crime--**

State v. Christy Pontiac-GMC, Inc., 354 N.W.2d 17 (Minn. 1984)

Facts. Christy Pontiac-GMC (D) is a corporation in the business of selling cars. In the spring of 1981, General Motors offered a cash rebate program to dealers for each car sold during the rebate period. The evidence shows that employees of D twice forged customer signatures to obtain and pocket for the dealership the customer's portion of the rebate. One of the salesmen who did the forgeries was convicted of theft in a separate trial. D was found guilty of theft and forgery and appeals.

Issue. Can a corporation be held criminally liable for a specific intent crime?

Held. Yes. Judgment affirmed.

- The legislature has not specifically excluded corporations from criminal liability. Therefore, its intent is for corporations to be considered persons.
- A corporation can be liable in civil tort for libel, assault and battery, and fraud. Therefore, it follows that corporations may be guilty of specific intent crimes.
- For a corporation to be liable, it must be clear that the activity was not an aberration of an employee acting on his own; the activity must reflect corporate policy.
- The jury must be satisfied beyond a reasonable doubt that the actions of the individual agent constitute the acts of the corporation.

- A corporation may be found liable for the acts of an agent if:

  (i) The agent was acting within the scope of employment;

  (ii) The agent was acting in furtherance of the corporation's business interest; and

  (iii) The criminal acts were authorized, ratified, or tolerated by the corporation.

- The elements will generally be proven by circumstantial evidence.

- The corporation may be found to be criminally liable even if the acts were expressly forbidden by corporate policy if it can be shown that those in positions of managerial authority acted or failed to act in such a way that it can be said that the act was ratified, tolerated, or authorized by the corporation.

XII. THEFT

A. CATEGORIES OF THEFT

The theft offenses were developed over a period of time as the criminal law expanded to include nonforcible, as will as forcible, appropriations of property. The offenses include larceny, embezzlement, and obtaining another's property by false pretenses. The underlying harm is the unpermitted acquisition of another's property.

B. LARCENY

1. Introduction.

a. **Elements.** The elements of larceny are: (i) a trespassory (ii) taking and (iii) carrying away of (iv) the personal property (v) of another (vi) with the intent to permanently deprive the owner of possession of the property. This offense is primarily an interference with the possessory rights of another. The taking is trespassory when it is done without the consent of the owner.

b. **Asportation.** This taking and carrying away of the property of another is usually held to mean that some acquisition of control or dominion over the property is necessary.

1) Possession or control need only be slight; that is, the length of time may be short, and the distance moved need not be far.

2) Thus, it is sufficient asportation where a thief lifts a person's wallet from his pocket but is detected and drops it before it is removed entirely. All that is required is the entire shifting of the property from the place it occupied.

c. **Trespass.** Larceny is a crime involving trespass (unlawful taking) from the possession of another. Possession does not necessarily require ownership. This taking can occur by the defendant himself or through an innocent agent (a person unaware of the facts *e.g.*, a young child); but the taking must not be by violence or force from the person of another, or the crime is robbery. In any event, if the person came into possession of property, there was no trespass (and thus no larceny).

1) **Larceny by trick or device.** In larceny by trick, the person receives goods from another with the latter's consent, but this consent is not valid to impart possession because it is derived by trick, fraud, or other unlawful device. This differs from the case of fraud

in that the intent to take the goods exists at the time possession is obtained.

a) **Example.** A convinces B to let him take B's camera "to show it to my wife," but A has the intent to steal it and does so on obtaining possession. This is larceny by trick or device.

2) **Distinguished from false pretenses.** Distinguishing larceny by trick or device from false pretenses, which is discussed *infra*, can be difficult.

d. **Grand and petit larceny.** When jurisdictions make this distinction, usually petit larceny is only a misdemeanor even though all of the elements for the crime are the same as for grand larceny. The difference relates to the fair market value of the goods that are taken (value under a certain amount being petit larceny).

2. **Actus Reus.**

a. **Trespassory taking and carrying away.** In *Lee v. State*, 474 A.2d 537 (Md. Ct. Spec. App. 1984), the court explained that theft-related offenses grew out of a concern for crimes of violence and later expanded to include the nonviolent taking of another's property—larceny. Initially, larceny required a trespassory taking and focused on the physical aspect of taking and obtaining possession. Thus, if an owner gave someone temporary possession of his property, the person receiving temporary possession (*e.g.*, a bailee) had possessorial immunity and could not be guilty of larceny even if he used the property in an unauthorized manner. In time, courts broadened the offense of larceny to include such misappropriation.

1) **Physical versus constructive possession--**

Rex v. Chisser, 83 Eng. Rep. 142 (King's Bench 1678).

Facts. Chisser (D) went to a shop and asked to see two crevats. When the shop owner placed the items in his hands, D immediately ran out of the shop with the merchandise.

Issue. Does a store customer commit a crime if he leaves a store with goods handed to him by the store owner before contracting to buy them?

Held. Yes.

♦ Although the shop owner delivered the crevats into D's hands, the goods were not out of her possession at the time of the delivery. The goods would remain in her possession until such time as a contract of sale was perfected.

---

2) **Possession versus custody--**

United States v. Mafnas, 701 F.2d 83 (9th Cir. 1983).

Facts. Mafnas (D) was employed by an armored car service which was hired to transport bags of money for banks. On three occasions, D opened bags and removed money. He was convicted of stealing money under 18 U.S.C. §2113(b), which makes it a crime to steal money belonging to a bank. D appeals.

Issue. Did D have lawful possession of the bags when he removed the money?

Held. No. Judgment affirmed.

- ♦ Section §2113(b) applies only to common law larceny, which requires a trespassory taking. D argues that he had lawful possession of the bags, with the consent of the banks, when he removed the money. However, the law distinguishes between possession and custody. If someone receives property for a limited or temporary purpose, he acquires only custody. Thus, if he keeps the property for himself, he commits larceny.

- ♦ D was entrusted with the money bags for delivery and had only temporary custody. The banks maintained constructive possession of the money bags until D delivered them. Taking the money went beyond the consent of the banks and constituted larceny. Even if D acted as a bailee, he is guilty of larceny because he opened the money bags, and a bailee who "breaks bulk" commits larceny.

---

3) **Owner's knowledge and assistance in the taking--**

Topolewski v. State, 109 N.W. 1037 (Wis. 1906).

Facts. Topolewski (D) arranged with a man who owed him money and was an employee of a packing company to place three barrels of meat on the loading platform for D to pick up and take away as though he were a customer. The employee informed the company and it told him to feign cooperation. D took the barrels; he was prosecuted for larceny and convicted. He appeals.

Issue. Is there a trespassory taking when the owner knew the goods were going to be taken and he facilitated the taking?

Held. No. Judgment reversed.

- The element of trespass did not exist. Trespass is lacking when the company allows its property to be taken regardless of the intent of the accused. By telling its employee to place the property on the platform for a man who would come to get it, the company consented to the taking. The company aided the commission of the offense.

---

4) **Larceny by trick--**

Rex v. Pear, 168 Eng. Rep. 208 (Central Criminal Court 1779).

Facts. Pear (D) hired a horse from a livery stable, stating that he would take the horse for a day journey and return it at eighth o'clock that evening. D provided a false address to the livery stable keeper. After acquiring the horse, D sold the horse to a third party. The jury found that D had hired the horse using fraud and had intended to sell it immediately.

Issue. Was D's conversion of the horse a mere breach of trust rather than a felonious conversion?

Held. No.

- If the jury believed that D intended to use the horse for a journey but was subsequently tempted to sell the horse, D would have to be acquitted. However, the jury found that D acted fraudulently and that the journey was a pretense to get the horse in D's possession so that he could sell it. Thus, the delivery of the horse by the stable keeper to D did not change the nature of the possession of the horse at the time of conversion, and D is guilty of a felony.

---

5) **Lost property--**

Brooks v. State, 35 Ohio St. 46 (1878).

Facts. While working, Brooks (D) found a roll of bank bills in the amount of $200 on the ground near a public hitching post. D did not let his fellow workers know of his finding. Three weeks before this event, the owner of the bills had posted notice of his loss in local newspapers. Evidence was given at trial that, after finding the bills, D found the roll he quit his job, spent some of the money on himself and his wife, and subsequently left town. There was no evidence that D was aware of the newspaper notices regarding the lost bills. D was convicted of larceny and appeals.

Issue. Does a finder of lost property have a legal obligation to seek out the owner before taking possession of the property if he has reason to believe that the owner can be found?

Held. Yes. Judgment affirmed.

- The owner of property retains title and constructive possession even if the property is lost. If a finder of property takes possession of it for his own use, he is guilty of trespass unless he can show that the property had been abandoned by the owner.

- Moreover, if the nature of the property and the circumstances under which it is found give the finder reason to believe that the owner can be found, but he nevertheless takes possession with the intent to appropriate the property to his own use, he is guilty of larceny.

Dissent. D should not have been convicted because the owner of the bills had given up searching for them, D did not have notice of the lost bills and the owner, and there was no mark on the bills to indicate the owner. Although D violated a moral obligation, he was not criminally liable.

---

b. The personal property of another--

Lund v. Commonwealth, 232 S.E.2d 745 (Va. 1977)

Facts. Lund (D), a graduate student preparing his doctoral dissertation, used the university's computer operation time and the services of the computer center personnel without obtaining the proper authorization. After there were complaints from various departments that unauthorized charges were being made to their accounts, D was investigated, and a large number of computer cards and printouts were found in his apartment. At trial, D stated that he did not think that he had done anything wrong because he was working on his dissertation, and four faculty members testified in D's behalf. Nevertheless, D was found guilty of grand larceny. D appeals.

Issue. Does the taking of computer operation time and the unauthorized use of computer personnel services constitute larceny?

Held. No. Judgment reversed.

- Section 18.1-100 of the statute governing the crime of larceny provides that anyone who commits simple larceny, not from the person of another, of goods and chattels of $100 or more, is guilty of grand larceny. Section 18.1-118 provides that anyone who, by false pretense with intent to defraud, obtains money or property that may be the subject of larceny is guilty of larceny.

- D contends that his conviction cannot be upheld because there was no evidence that property was stolen or that the property involved had a value of $100 or more, and computer time and services are not the subject of larceny. We agree.

- At common law and under our larceny statutes, larceny involves the taking and carrying away of goods and chattels. Time and services cannot be taken and carried away. Thus, the term "goods and chattels" does not include computer operation time and the services of the computer center personnel. The taking must be of a concrete article of personal property. Therefore, the unauthorized use of a computer cannot be the subject of larceny.

- D cannot be convicted of grand larceny of items used to access the computer because there was no evidence that these items were stolen or that they had a market value of $100 or more. In addition, the computer printouts had no ascertainable monetary value to the university or the computer center.

Comment. One year after the *Lund* decision, the Virginia legislature enacted a statute providing that computer time or services could be the subject of larceny, embezzlement, or false pretenses.

---

3. Mens Rea.

a. **Introduction.** Specific intent is required for larceny. The taking has to be done with the specific intent to fraudulently and permanently deprive the possessor of his goods.

1) **Bona fide claim to possession.** A taking by A where A has a bona fide claim of right to possession is not larceny, even where A is actually wrong in his claim.

2) **Intent to take and abandon.** The intent to take property and then to abandon it without returning it to its owner is sufficient.

3) **Intent to take and use.** If the taker intends to just take and use the property and then to return it to the owner, it is not larceny. For example, there is no larceny when a person takes a car for a "joy ride" and then returns it.

4) **"Continuing trespass" doctrine.** At some point in time, the felonious intent must accompany the trespass to possession. However, it is not always required that there is such intent at the time the property is first taken. As long as the taking constitutes a trespass (albeit innocent or in good faith), the trespass "continues" as long as the defendant holds the goods, and if at any time thereafter he

forms the intent to steal them, there is then the concurrence of trespass and felonious intent, which constitutes the crime of larceny. For example, the defendant takes the goods of another in the honest, but mistaken, belief that he owns them (innocent trespass). Later he discovers that he does not, but decides to appropriate them anyway. He is guilty of larceny.

b. **Permanent taking requirement--**

People v. Brown, 38 P. 518 (Cal. 1894).

Facts. Brown (D), age 17, entered the house of a boy with whom he had had an argument, and took a bicycle, intending to return it later. Before he could return it, he was caught. D was convicted of burglary, committed in entering a house with the intent to commit grand larceny, after a jury instruction that indicated that all that needed to be shown was an intent to deprive the owner of possession temporarily. D appeals.

Issue. Is a taking of property without the intent to permanently deprive the owner of his rightful possession larceny?

Held. No. Judgment reversed.

- The jury instruction was incorrect. A felonious taking requires that the taking be with the intent to deprive the owner of possession permanently.

Comment. If the taker abandons the property or recklessly exposes it to loss, he may have had the intent to permanently deprive.

---

c. **The intent to steal property--**

People v. Davis, 965 P.2d 1165 (Cal. 1998)

Facts. Davis (D) entered a Mervyn's department store, carrying a Mervyn's shopping bag. D went to the men's department, took a shirt from its hanger, and carried it to the women's department on the other side of the store. He put the shirt on a sales counter and told the cashier that he had bought it for his father and wanted to return it because it did not fit his father. D said that he did not have a receipt since the shirt was a gift. A store security agent, who had been watching D, phoned the cashier and told her to issue a credit voucher to D. The cashier prepared the voucher, and D signed it, using a false name. As D walked away from the counter with the voucher, the security agent detained D. At trial, D was convicted of theft by larceny. D appeals.

Issue. Does a person commit larceny if he takes possession of the property of another just long enough to exchange it for a refund?

Held. Yes. Judgment affirmed.

- Theft by larceny is committed when a person (i) takes possession (ii) of personal property (iii) owned or possessed by another, (iv) by means of trespass and (v) with intent to steal the property, and (vi) carries the property away. In this case, D took possession of the shirt owned by Mervyn's and moved it sufficiently to satisfy the asportation requirement. However, by dividing his course of conduct into two distinct acts, D argues that the elements of trespass and intent to steal are missing.

- D contends that his first act was to take the shirt from the rack and carry it to the cash register. He claims that that act lacked the element of intent to steal because he intended to have possession only long enough to exchange the shirt for a refund and had no intent to permanently deprive Mervyn's of the shirt. D contends that his second act was to misrepresent to the cashier that he had bought the shirt at Mervyn's and to accept the credit voucher. D argues that the element of trespass was missing because the store, acting through its security agent, consented to the issuance of the voucher, knowing how D came into possession of the shirt. But the question is not whether Mervyn's consented to the issuance of the voucher; the question is whether Mervyn's consented to D's taking the shirt in the first place.

- Although D claims that he did not intend to deprive the store permanently of possession of the shirt, the requisite intent to steal has been found even though the defendant did not intend to deprive the owner permanently of possession when the defendant intended to: (i) sell the property back to its owner, (ii) claim a reward for finding the property, or (iii) as in this case, return the property to its owner for a refund. In each of these categories of cases, the defendant asserted a right of ownership when he claimed a right to sell the property back to its owner, receive a reward for its return, or receive a refund for it. Also, in each case, the defendant created a substantial risk to the owner of permanent loss because the property would not be returned unless the owner agreed to buy it or give a reward or refund for it.

- Such intent to claim ownership constitutes an intent to permanently deprive the owner of the property within the meaning of the law of larceny. Furthermore, Mervyn's did not consent to D's taking possession of the shirt with the intent to steal it. Therefore, D's conduct constituted a trespassory taking within the meaning of the law of larceny.

C. EMBEZZLEMENT

1. **Definition.** Embezzlement is the statutory offense involving the unlawful

and fraudulent appropriation of property by a person to whom it was entrusted.

2. **Elements of the Crime.**

a. **Intent.** The defendant must have the specific intent to permanently appropriate the property of another to use outside the scope of the trust that placed it in his possession. It is not embezzlement where the defendant takes the property in good faith under a bona fide claim of right, even though in fact the claim of right is untenable. There is no embezzlement where the defendant receives the money pursuant to a bona fide loan.

b. **Subject matter of embezzlement.** This is a question of statutory interpretation. Many statutes simply state "the property of another."

c. **Relationship of confidence or trust.** The property must have come into the defendant's possession as a result of his fiduciary relationship with the owner. This simply means that the defendant has possession by and for another.

d. **Possession.** Some courts have held that because embezzlement was meant to plug gaps in the crime of larceny, embezzlement will not lie unless the defendant has possession of the goods of another, as opposed to mere custody (because in this latter case, conversion will amount to larceny).

1) For example, if goods are delivered by the owner to his employee, there is only custody, and the employee's subsequent conversion can only be larceny.

2) But if a third person delivers money to the employee for the master, and the employee does not put it where he is instructed to put it but immediately converts it, he has possession and is thus guilty of embezzlement.

e. **Election.** Normally the prosecution will be required to elect whether it will proceed under the theory of larceny or embezzlement.

3. **Possession of Property by Employee--**

Rex v. Bazeley, 168 Eng. Rep. 517 (Central Criminal Court 1799).

Facts. Bazely (D), a bank teller, received a bank note from a customer and appropriated it to his own use instead of putting it into the bank's money drawer. D was charged with larceny.

Issue. Does a person commit larceny if he appropriates property to his own use before the rightful owner has possession of the property?

Held. No. Defendant acquitted.

- To constitute the crime of larceny, the property must be taken from the actual or constructive possession of the owner. The prosecution argues that the bank had constructive possession of the bank note because the possession in law follows the right of property. The prosecution contends that the note was not deposited with D as a matter of trust to him; it was paid at the counter of the bank of which D was merely an organ. We disagree because, although the bank had the right to the bank note, D intercepted it before it came into the bank's possession.

- Even if the bank did have possession of the note, there could be no felony unless D intended to steal the note at the time it came to his hands. D came into possession of the note lawfully, and there is no evidence that D had a felonious intent to steal it at the time the note came to his hands.

- Under the circumstances, D committed a breach of trust, but such a breach of trust was not a felony. As a result of this case, a statute, entitled "An Act to protect Masters and others against Embezzlement, by their Clerks or Servants," was passed.

D. FALSE PRETENSES

1. **Definition.** This crime involves a false representation with the intent to defraud the owner and is very similar to that of "larceny by trick or device," mentioned above. The difference is that false pretenses includes obtaining both posssession and ***title*** to property. [People v. Ingram, 76 Cal. Rptr. 2d 553 (Cal. Ct. App. 1998)] At common law, there was no crime where title was passed, so this crime was created by statute to remedy the gap in coverage. The elements of the crime are as follows:

    a. **Misrepresentation of a past or existing fact.** There must be some pretense or misrepresentation. This may occur in the form of words or conduct. Mere failure to disclose facts is not usually sufficient.

        1) **Future events.** A statement by the defendant as to future events, as opposed to past or existing facts, is not usually sufficient. Therefore, prediction, promises, dealer's talk, or "puffing" do not represent actionable misrepresentations.

        2) **Opinions.** Similarly, mere expression of "opinion" or "belief" is not wrong; but some courts have held that the defendant is guilty

of misrepresenting his state of mind or intention (a "fact") when he expresses an intention (as to perform or do something in the future) and does not really have that intention.

b. **Intent to defraud.** The facts represented must in fact be false ones, and the defendant must have knowledge of this falsity and the specific intent to permanently deprive the owner of his property. The intent to just use the property is not sufficient.

c. **Reliance.** The misrepresentation must be such that a reasonable person would have relied on it; and, in fact, the owner of the property must have relied on it.

d. **Title.** The owner must intend to part with complete ownership and title to the property, not just possession. This is a fine distinction from the crime of larceny.

e. **Example.** If A promises (with intent to defraud) to sell and deliver goods to B that are not in existence, B pays for them in advance, and A never delivers the goods, false pretenses will lie.

2. **Reliance on Misrepresentation--**

People v. Whight, 43 Cal. Rptr. 2d 163 (Cal. Ct. App. 1995).

Facts. Whight (D) opened a checking account and was issued an ATM card. Six months later, his account was overdrawn, and the bank closed the account. The ATM card should have also been canceled and revoked, but due to a computer error, D was still able to use his ATM card at four Safeway stores. Within two months, D obtained over $19,000 in cash, using his ATM card at those stores. He was convicted of four counts of grand theft by false pretenses.

Issue. Did the stores rely on D's presentation of his ATM card as valid?

Held. Yes. Judgment affirmed.

- For a conviction of theft by false pretenses, it must be shown that: (i) the defendant made a false representation, (ii) the representation was made with the intent to defraud the owner of his property, and (iii) the owner parted with his property in reliance on the representation. The representation need not be made as an oral or written statement; it may consist of conduct and may be express or implied. Also, the reliance on the false representation may be inferred from the evidence.

- When D proffered his ATM card at the stores, he implied that the card was valid. D argues that the store employees did not just give him cash because he presented the card, but relied on the computer system to verify the card. Reliance on the false representation may be lacking if: (i) the owner knew that the representation was false, or did not believe it was true; (ii) the owner did not rely on the false representation, but investigated for himself or sought and relied on other advice; (iii) the owner parted with his property for reasons other than the false representation or in reliance on other representations not shown to be false.

- D claims that the causal chain of reliance was broken because Safeway used a computer authorization system to investigate whether D should have been approved and did not rely solely on D's representation. However, the false pretense need not have been the only reason that an owner parted with his property, but it must have materially influenced the owner to do so. Furthermore, the record established that Safeway did not rely on computer authorization. When a Safeway store does not get authorization in a reasonable amount of time, it will "stand in" for the transaction and resubmit the transaction at a later time for approval. This is done for customer service. Because of a glitch in the computer system concerning D's account, Safeway received a code indicating that there was no response and treated D's transactions as "stand-ins." Safeway relied only on D's implicit representation that his card was valid; the element of reliance was established.

E. FEDERAL MAIL, WIRE, AND COMPUTER FRAUD

1. Unathorized Access Not a Felony--

United States v. Czubinski, 106 F.3d 1069 (1st Cir. 1997).

Facts. Czubinski (D) was a Contact Representative for the IRS. To answer taxpayers' questions regarding their returns, D had access to a computer system known as the Integrated Data Retrieval System ("IDRS") and could retrieve income tax return information regarding virtually any taxpayer. In 1992, D conducted numerous unauthorized searches of IDRS files and looked at confidential information regarding the tax returns of taxpayers, including: two individuals involved in the David Duke presidential campaign, an assistant district attorney who had been prosecuting D's father on an unrelated felony, a police officer who was involved in a community organization with one of D's brothers, and a woman D had dated a few times. At trial, the government's only evidence that D had any intent to use the confidential information for wrongful ends was the testimony of Murray, an acquaintance of D who briefly participated in D's local KKK chapter and worked with D on the David Duke campaign. Murray testified that D had stated that he intended to use some of the information to create dossiers on people involved in the white supremacist movement. However, there was no evidence that D took steps toward making the dossiers or that he shared any of the information that he accessed. Nevertheless, D was convicted on nine counts of wire fraud and four counts of computer fraud. D appeals.

Issue. Does unauthorized access of a federal interest computer with the intent only to retrieve information to satisfy one's curiosity constitute wire fraud or computer fraud?

Held. No. Judgment reversed.

- To support a conviction for wire fraud, the government must prove two elements beyond a reasonable doubt: (i) the defendant's knowing and willing participation in a scheme or artifice to defraud, with the specific intent to defraud; and (ii) the use of interstate wire communications in furtherance of the scheme. In this case, the government argued that: (i) D defrauded the IRS of its property by acquiring confidential information for certain intended personal uses, violating 18 U.S.C. section 1343; and (ii) D defrauded the IRS and the public of their intangible right to honest services, violating 18 U.S.C. section 1346.

- Confidential information may constitute intangible property, and its unauthorized dissemination or other use may deprive the owner of its property rights. However, merely accessing confidential information, without intending to do more, is not a deprivation of property under the wire fraud statute. There must also be the intent to deprive the owner of property and to use the interstate wire transmissions to accomplish a scheme to defraud (even if it is not successfully carried out) for a conviction of wire fraud under section 1343. D did not create dossiers or even take steps toward creating them, and no evidence suggests that D shared taxpayer information with others. Because there is no evidence that D used or intended to use the taxpayer information other than to satisfy his curiosity, an intent to deprive cannot be proven, and thus a scheme to defraud has not been shown.

- As for the government's allegation of a section 1346 violation, a scheme to deprive another of the right to honest services typically involves serious corruption, such as embezzlement of public funds or bribery of public officials, but it does not encompass all official misconduct that results in the official's personal gain. A public official cannot be convicted unless his wrongdoing deprived the public of its right to his honest services and was intended to do so. D was not bribed, did not embezzle funds, and did not receive or intend to receive any tangible benefit. The IRS did not inform D that his wrongdoing would be punishable by anything more than dismissal; all governmental workplace violations should not be transformed into felonies. The government did not prove that D deprived, or intended to deprive, the public or the IRS of their right to his honest services or that he failed to carry out his official tasks adequately or intended to do so.

- Regarding the claim of computer fraud, section 1030(a)(4) of the Computer Fraud and Abuse Act prohibits the unauthorized access of a federal interest computer with the intent to defraud and to wrongly obtain something of value from another. However, the government failed to show that D obtained anything of value, and section 1030 does not punish mere unauthorized access.

- We caution that although D's membership in a white supremacist group may be morally offensive, the wire fraud statute must not be used as a vehicle for prosecuting only those individuals whose views are disdained.

Comment. The federal mail fraud statute is similar to the wire fraud statute, but it covers schemes to defraud by using a post office or authorized mail depository to send something to be delivered by the Postal Service.

TABLE OF CASES

(Page numbers of briefed cases in bold)

NOTES

NOTES

NOTES

NOTES

NOTES

NOTES